Janice Houser

40 Mile!

Tales of an Alaskan
Gold Mining Woman

Dedication

To all those who share my passion for the search,
especially Kurt and Rich.

****

Table of Contents

1. Definition of Terms

BLM: Bureau of Land Management. Part of the Department of the Interior, it oversees the mining in our Mining District. Federal Government.

DNR: Division of Mining. Department of Natural Resources. Part of the State of Alaska, DNR is where the records of State of Alaska claims are kept.

DOT: Department of Transportation.

OZT: Troy ounce, the weighing system for precious metals. One troy ounce is 31.1 grams. A regular or avoirdupois ounce, used, for example, to weigh broccoli or humans, is 28 grams.

Dredge: The machine used to suck up and start concentrating the gold.

Dredgers: The people involved with the dredge.

Cat Mining: The method of pushing dirt into a concentrating cleanup system using dozers and other heavy equipment.

MP: Milepost. The highway mile markers.

Pan of Fine Gold. This is about 35 ounces

State of Alaska, marked in red

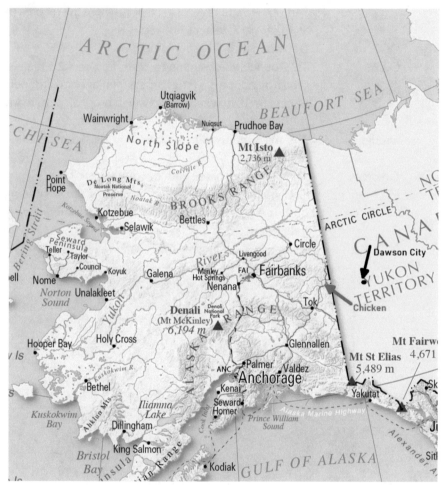

Alaska
(map: courtesy of nationsonline.org)

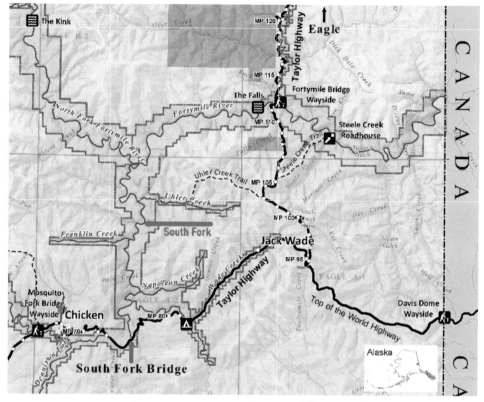

*The section of the American 40 Mile River
where most dredging occurred.*

*(Map based on an extract from a map by the BLM:
https://www.blm.gov/documents/alaska/public-
room/map/fortymile-wild-and-scenic-river-taylor-highway-
georeferenced-pdf)*

2. INTRODUCTION

From May 1980 until September 1995, I actively gold mined on all three forks of the 40 Mile River in remote Alaska, near the town of Chicken.

Here's the story of how a 36-year-old woman used to living in cities found herself face-to-face with few amenities, in a tent, for a summer, in what became the career of a lifetime. In a man's world. In a bear's world. Alaska. Gold.

What follows is a compilation of letters, journals, technical information on suction dredges (not too much!), memories, and photos designed to inform and entertain. All numbers, facts, or other memories are mine to the best of my ability to remember. You might hear different versions of these events elsewhere. You be the judge. But this is how I remember my grand adventure on the 40 Mile River in the early days of modern portable suction dredging, a method of gold mining.

A number of books have been written about gold mining on the 40 Mile River. Until now, none has been about the dredgers. Here is a look at a modern method of gold extraction: the portable suction dredge, along with the dredgers (the people who run the dredges), and the attendant lifestyle.

Michael Gates, in *Gold at Fortymile Creek: Early Days in the Yukon,* used "Fortymile" for the name of the river and "Forty Mile" for the town that sprang up in 1886 at the river's confluence with the Yukon River. The BLM also spells the river's name as one word.

As this info was not on my radar when I learned another way in my early days, I have the name of the river in my mind as 40 Mile. Please indulge this spelling. Most of today's American portable dredge mining has been done in parts of the river system that did not see many of the old-timers. We lost touch with the other end of the river, which is in Canada, and at the same time, lost earliest history, including the spelling of its name.

I did a search for "40 Mile." I found a diversity of companies using some version of the name, such as 40 Mile Air. Indeed, many American miners reference the 40 Mile River, and the government sometimes calls the Fortymile caribou herd by the name 40 Mile caribou herd. I read a book called, *Chicken, Alaska* subtitled *Then and Now,* by Caryl Hanks, in which she spells the river Forty Mile. Recently, I saw an old map of the Forty-Mile River, which also called it Cone Hill River and Schwatka River.

I guess we should not be too surprised at this confusion. Many of us know the Chicken and ptarmigan story that goes: The turn-of-the-century miners wanted to name their community after the numerous ptarmigan, a type of grouse. They could not agree on the spelling. The government came in and said, "Everyone can spell Chicken, which the ptarmigan resembles. We will name it Chicken."

So, 40 Mile it is, in this story of a river and the people who live there and love it.

In 2023, long after I wrote this, a dredger brought me a photo which sets it all in perspective:

Mining district building in Chicken, AK. And here is how we spell it. Writ large. Photo by James Putman.

The 40 Mile River is so remote it is challenging to convey how "out there" it is, but I am going to try.

The nearest civilization to Chicken and the 40 Mile River is pretty much in the middle of nowhere itself, a place called Tok (pronounced "Toke"). Tok is a town of about 1250 people. It has stores, restaurants, and gas stations, with year-round jobs and electricity, phones, and running water.

By road, Tok is 200 miles southeast of Fairbanks or 325 miles northeast of Anchorage where the two roads from these two big cities meet, then run east as one toward the Canadian border in Interior Alaska. When Tok was established in 1943 as a maintenance center for the Alaska Highway, it was named Tok Junction because the two highways meet there.

The nearest town of Tok's size, Delta Junction, is 95 miles west toward Fairbanks, giving another idea of Tok's isolation. If you are going south, you will have to drive 141 miles to Glenallen for a same size town.

Leaving all these Tok services behind, head east toward the Canadian border. Go 12 miles. Turn left at Tetlin Junction heading north on the unpaved, potholed, one-and-a-half lane, blind-cornered Taylor Highway through miles and miles of scenery with no facilities of any kind. Proceed to milepost (hereinafter referred to as MP) 67 which is Chicken, with a post office and a summertime bar. The bar, back in the early 1980s, sometimes had a few cans of Spam, some eggs of questionable age, a loaf of bread—often green around the edges, and possibly a jar of mayonnaise past its expiration date, any of which we would probably buy, glad to have it. Through Chicken to MP 75, South Fork bridge. Unload truck. Carry to boat. Load boat. Head downriver, a trip which can take hours, even without mishaps. Unload boat. Make as many trips as it takes.

So, don't forget to pick up all you think you want while in Tok because it is a long way back to get that toothpaste, for instance! Once, I was fretting over the price of a specialty chocolate bar being too expensive in the store in Tok when Rich (my third mining partner) put it into perspective: On the river, it would be worth every penny of the price and much more.

3. Cast of Characters

JANICE HOUSER: I wanted my name in this list, along with everyone else's.

LEE FUEL: My first mining partner, from Memphis. Used to living a very basic and outdoor lifestyle. He adapted easily, cheerfully sitting on stumps around a smoky campfire trying to stay warm. Also, volatile. And kind of lazy about the whole work thing. No matter because it was to this man I hitched my star. Virtually no disaster held him back for long.

CAROLE LARSON: My friend since 1976 in Memphis. She lived across the street in 1980. We jogged together and talked. Ultimately, she decided to go mining with Lee and me for the first few weeks. At the time, our knowledge of mining was so sketchy, we thought we would just go and pick up the nuggets off the ground without any learning curve.

MAIK SCHLUROFF: Longtime friend from Southern Germany on the Swiss border in the city of Konstanz. His name is pronounced "Mike." Lee and I attempted to convince Maik to go mining with us, but he had other plans. Lucky for him because it would be years before all the kinks were worked out of the gold mining experience. Two people dealing with this turned out to be enough for those early years.

WALTER PARTRIDGE: Soulmate friend in Memphis. I wrote a letter to him from the goldfields, which I have included here.

KURT HOUSER: My brother and second mining partner. When I began mining, he was living in Spokane, WA, age 24. He came up to 40 Mile and got gold fever, which wound up occupying his life for the next 30 years. He dredged on the prospecting dredge with Rich and me, as well as working with other dredgers along the way or on his own. He also worked Cat mining during his time there and lived a bunch of winters in the cabin three and a half miles from Chicken.

RICH GOODSON: My third mining partner. I met Rich early in my mining career when Lee and I were at the South Fork bridge. Rich was with his brother, Gary, and long-time friend Clyde Miles, down by the river, panning. I remember Rich from that day, but more awareness would come later because for a while I was more interested in what Gary had to say. Then Rich's deep interest in all things gold won me over. He has mined on the 40 Mile River and in Nome. He began in 1977 and was still dredging in the 40 Mile in 2023 at the age of 77.

GARY GOODSON, JOE TAYLOR, and CLYDE MILES: These three guys worked with Rich for most of the mining years. Gary, Rich's brother, Clyde, Rich's friend from youth, and Joe, a friend from Fairbanks with a very cheerful disposition were responsible for producing most of the big quantities of gold that Rich put them onto. These discoveries were mostly a result of Rich's prospect panning on spots he thought would be a hot spot. My brother's and my part in all this was dredge prospecting along with Rich, locating the gold for these guys to dredge up.

WES and RANDY DEVORE: Showed up on 40 Mile in 1984. We first encountered them down below Napoleon Creek, on the straightaway, setting up their 8″ dredge. It was love at first sight. These two brothers seemed like teddy bears but were made of steel and got things done. They were early to

the 40 Mile with hovercrafts, hovercraft dredges, and that huge fold-out, mostly cleanup, backhoe 5″ dredge, referred to by the dredging

community as Chitty Chitty Bang Bang. Wes is a superior fabricator and visionary, while Randy helps with the fabricating by being Johnny-on-the-spot with needed things while Wes welds and plans. Randy excels at organization and paying attention to the details. They, too, are still dredging. Wes is 83, Randy 77. Wes once said he wants to die with his wetsuit on.

We have shared many adventures in the 39 years I have known them. They have been dredging in the Bering Sea in Nome, Alaska since 2007 or so. We have many 40 Mile-and-beyond memories and are still making more, thanks to modern communications. Wes's wife, Judy, and their son, Doug, spent parts of several summers in 40 Mile country.

JUDD and GAIL (MURPHY) EDGERTON: From Palmer, AK, they came to Napoleon Creek in 1992 to Cat mine, after starting out at Robinson Creek in 1990. With great determination and success, they have worked the whole valley in an impressively complete, organized way. Somehow, they managed to find the time to be President and Secretary of the 40 Mile Mining Association for a long time. Much of the time since they first came, they have spent the winter, raising their two boys, Derek and David, out there. I always say they set high standards in the neighborhood when they moved to Napoleon Creek, with their huge cabin built of logs from the valley, their airstrip, and their efficient method of mining.

ARIADNE (ARI) WIREN: Ari was a special woman and a highly esteemed friend. When she retired from her career in finance in Philadelphia and moved to Chicken with Greg and Susan (son and daughter-in-law), she entered a whole new phase of her amazing life, living out there on her own for 17 years as part of the year-round population.

GREG and SUSAN WIREN: Ari's son and his wife came to the 40 Mile because of his gold dreams, then stayed because Susan, the more practical one, seized the opportunity in 1989 to buy Beautiful Downtown Chicken: cafe, gas, bar, liquor store, and mercantile emporium. Greg left some years later, moving to France. Susan is still rocking it with their sons, Max and Wolfgang, both of whom she carried around on her back in a baby sling while rolling out the dough at 6 a.m. for her fresh chicken noodle soup, famous cinnamon rolls and other delectable food for the day, plus coffee for the miners. She's done the 6 a.m. thing, every day, every summer, cooking, serving, and selling truly awesome meals. She put the recipes into her cookbook entitled *I Don't Do Chainsaws*. In recent years, Max has taken over the business.

ROGER TALLINI: Roger was a superman. He set the record while running an 8" dredge by himself: 140 ozt and 647 hours underwater, both in one season.  Extraordinary. When Roger was dealing with clogs in the dredge hose, he turned off the clock! He made sure he put his time in; he was a very driven person. It is hard to imagine anyone doing more, especially on such worked-over ground. Other summers, he was disguised as an ordinary dredger, partnering up with various regulars. Roger summed it all up when he said, "My overriding memory was how much I enjoyed the life, the peace, the freedom and independence of mining. From age 35-50 (the heart of life), I followed my heart." Most of us on the river said the same thing.

RUDD VAN DYNE: Rudd came to the Mainstem in 1991. He reminded me of Rich in his  single-minded pursuit of gold. I would say he was the most successful dredger after Rich left for Nome. Rudd continued his production through today, a time when there is less gold left in the bottom of the river. Every year he keeps his focus and mines. He was still mining in 2021.

CHRIS MARSHALL: Rich and I met Chris when he rented us the shop in Tok. He became one of my best friends. His background of spending summers in his youth dredging with his father in northern California paved the way for gold dreams in Alaska.

Chris is a master fabricator and welder. He builds Burner Units, mostly for remote Native villages' trash problem resolution, as well as being a firefighter, an auto and airplane mechanic, carpenter, and highway landowner, including the Alaskan Stoves Campground and the Alaskan Stoves Hostel. He is much more, in the way of the frontiersmen and women. Now that I have written it, I wonder how he

16

has the time to do all this. He lives in Tok year-round, with his two rescue dogs from Kabul, Afghanistan, and his rescue cat from Tok.

COLT: Kurt's dog. Usually referred to as Doogie and sometimes, when we were annoyed with him, we called him Doogie Houser. But his official name is Colt. He was in camp with us, keeping us entertained, doing his dog thing.

The list is long. More characters are listed at the end of this book.

4. HOW IT BEGAN

Memphis, TN. January 16, 1980

I wasn't always a gold miner. I had a comfortable routine of job, friends, and the American dream, without any conscious desire to change where I was in my Memphis life. If I had had a desire to change, I would not have come up with what actually happened if I had thought of the wildest possibilities I could imagine. Even when I agreed to the subsequent plan, I had no real idea what I was agreeing to.

I didn't know how much my life was about to change when I went to answer the knock on the door.

There stood Lee Fuel, a former neighbor I had not seen in five years. "Uh oh, trouble," I thought, remembering his reputation of temper tantrums. Still, it was daylight, and my next-door neighbor, Paul, was home. Lee seemed calm enough to me. After talking to him a few moments through the screen door, I let him in.

We talked for a while before he got to the reason for his visit. He asked me if I wanted to go gold mining in Alaska, to which I answered "no."

Undeterred, he went on. "We could retire on a sailboat in the Caribbean."

Well, now you are talking. I said, "Tell me more."

There was not any consideration on my part about whether I wanted to retire on a sailboat or with this guy. The plan sounded great so far when set in the beautiful waters of the Caribbean with shiny nuggets being part of the picture. Although I pretty much always get seasick in a boat on the ocean, I didn't think of it at the time. I didn't question why everybody wasn't doing it either.

He needed an investor. All reservation was swept away by a force larger than I (gold fever which I caught in a flash!). Or maybe I was just ready for adventure. I found myself enthusiastically committing $7,500 to this quest for the golden dream while having a summer escape.

On January 17, I awoke with a nervous twitch, wondering whether I had really agreed to give Lee the first $1,000 that day. When he came to get it, I was asleep again. I could not fully wake up when he knocked. I passed the money through the door and went back to bed.

We spent the next four months getting a truck, boat, boat motor, camping gear, and an 8" dredge. Since the price of gold was at an all-time high that year, many people were thinking as we were thinking. They were also buying dredges to go seek their fortunes. The main dredge maker was backordering, so in March, we had to prepay the $8,000 for the dredge, to be picked up in Los Angeles, CA, on our way North to Alaska in late May.

Even if you are not much of a mathematician, you can see we were already more than doubling the initial estimate of the cost. But no matter. We were off to make our fortunes and dreaming of the Caribbean. Talk about counting chickens.

Here is the story of how we got the truck:

There once was a truck, a 10-year-old, school bus yellow and white, 1970 Ford F-250 Camper Special, that passed an unknown amount of time hanging out in a pasture in rural Western Tennessee. With its engine needing an overhaul, it did not seem to have much of a future ahead.

My fabulous truck: 1970 F250 Ford Camper Special after we had used it for two years on the Taylor Highway

Then, along came Lee Fuel in February 1980, needing a truck and an overhaul on his future. In a match made in heaven, they were teamed up, along with Janice, to follow their entangled destinies.

Lee had attended a vocational school and managed to get on the list there to have the students rebuild the truck's engine, as well as lots of other areas to be checked and fixed, such as the brakes, clutch, power steering, and exhaust system and anything else the students found. Yay!

I wasn't the only one overlooking Lee's true character. Maik (pronounced "Mike") Schluroff, my friend from Germany, wrote about his first meeting with Lee:

Just a few days before my longtime friend Janice left with Lee and her friend Carole for the big adventure of going gold hunting in Alaska, I met up with Janice and Lee in Memphis, Tennessee. I was on my way from Los Angeles via MIT back to my hometown Konstanz in southern Germany. Unfortunately, I had but a few hours to spend until my plane left. We sat down for a good cup of tea to get acquainted and decide on what to do in those few hours.

Lee turned out to be an open, easy-going guy of many talents, who loved his personal freedom, knew a lot about motors, hunting and animals, and appeared to be a very open and honest person. Having always been an anti-military person, I was quite surprised to learn that Lee had served in the Navy. To me, that didn't go at all with his love of freedom and independence or with his gentle manner.

"How the heck did someone like you get into the Navy?"

"Well," Lee replied, "friends of mine talked me into raiding a kiosk. What I didn't know and wouldn't have approved of, was that they had a gun with them. We got caught and the judge gave me a choice of either a five-year term in jail or volunteering for the Navy."

"In the Navy they must have broken your personality."

Lee told me, "They certainly harassed me, but they didn't break me. For example, the captain of the ship I was on had a first-class rifleman in his crew, who he intended to send to the annual shooting competition between the Navy, Air Force and Army. For this purpose, he had set up a practice shooting range on the ship, where this guy practiced his marksmanship all the time. I was, as usual, busy scrubbing the deck."

"I hollered to him: "Hey guy, your shooting is poor. You wouldn't even hit a bear if it was standing in front of you."

"The guy tried to ignore me because he could not believe that a Seaman 3rd Class could be that daring to a higher rank. I kept pestering him until he told me to come up for a shootout."

"If you shoot better than I do, I'll forget about it. If not, I'll have you arrested," the shooter said.

"So, we shot. I shot three rings more than he. He had me arrested anyway, but I only had to be in the brig for one day."

It was time then to decide what to do with the remaining few hours of my stay in Memphis. Janice suggested the best salad bar in town, but Lee had other ideas. "Let's take out the truck for a test ride and then shoot the gun."

As a die-hard peacenik I shunned the idea of firing a gun, but something in me said: "You have never in your life fired a gun. So, try it."

We took the truck down into the wilderness alongside the Mississippi River. Lee pointed out to me plants, trees, and animals, and made me listen to the sounds of the outdoors, instructing me to draw conclusions from the sounds as to where and which animal would be around the next corner.

We did some joyriding on the sandbar where we got stuck as completely as sand can do. Janice and I got a lesson in digging out a stuck truck, while Lee leaned back against a tree, barking instructions.

Lee then picked an old tree, gave me a few instructions, and let me shoot at the tree. As the rifle, a Marlin 45-70, was rather heavy–it was intended to stop a grizzly dead in its tracks, I was mostly busy with preparing for the recoil.

Oh wow, what a power! Very dangerous. One could get addicted to that feeling of power. Draws you into a very atavistic region of your brain. That experience has stuck with me ever since. Curiously enough, the next time I had a rifle in my hands was 34 years later, when I met Janice again at her summer home at Tok, Alaska.

I was duly impressed by this shooting lesson. My curiosity about Lee's naval career was not yet satisfied. I wondered again whether the Navy had broken Lee, but he replied that he had spent a lot of time scrubbing the deck and in the brig, yet had not changed his defiant manner.

21

Lee continued the story: "After several weeks at sea, we arrived at an Asian seaport. Everybody was eager to leave the ship and enjoy the shore leave. I, of course, had to stay onboard and scrub the deck. Our ship was moored at the far end of a huge pier. When the crew returned from their shore leave late at night with most of them drunk, they rounded the corner and saw our ship, where someone in giant letters had painted FOR SALE."

I have included this remembrance to point out how charismatic and deceiving Lee was. All through this account, there are clues to his troublemaking abilities, but the overriding impression is one of competence. His talents were so different from most of the people I knew that I confused his abilities with accomplishment. Plus, there was that pesky gold fever clouding my judgment.

5. LETTERS TO MAIK, WALTER & CAROLE

May 17, 1980

Dear Maik,

We began our trip 24 hours ago. The stress and strain have been rampant ever since. Carole Larson, my neighbor, decided to go with us for a few weeks and help pick up the nuggets. After weeks of jogging together during which I talked about the mining trip, she wanted to go too.

Carole, Lee, and I got up at 6 a.m. yesterday to load the truck. By 2 p.m., we had stuffed every nook and cranny. I would find out when we loaded the dredge in L.A. that I didn't know much about nooks and crannies. We added the dredge into the mix somehow. We looked like the Beverly Hillbillies! Our stuff was piled up sky high on the back of the truck. I have never seen anything like it in real life. After various goodbyes, we hit the road.

We left our watches at home and became the kind of people nature intended, not the kind caught up in the 9-5 and constant TV. Our pace, set by urges, not schedules, set us free. If we wanted to stop three times in 30 minutes, we did.

We did not have to be anywhere at any arranged time until Monday when we were to pick up the dredge in L.A.

Lee demanded to drive all the way to Alaska since the truck was full of our irreplaceable equipment. I guess neither Carole nor I could be trusted. Of course, it is replaceable, but a wreck could wipe us out. He drove 24 hours, more or less straight through, aided (or hindered) by speed, beer and cigarettes. By 3 a.m. he was a terror. Being so stressed out from fatigue and drugs, he provoked outrage from both Carole and me, making matters even worse. This caused me to wonder how his driving was any safer than either Carole's or mine might have been.

He was ready to leave us with the truck; he was threatening both of us with physical harm. Finally, just before we threw him to the dogs, no longer able to ignore his hallucinations and physical exhaustion, he pulled the truck off the road and fell asleep within minutes.

I imagine Carole had a lot to think about since this was her first encounter with Lee's negative strength, which could be disquieting under the "best" conditions but was intimidating and overwhelming today. Or maybe not; she also fell asleep quickly.

I sat outside, enjoying the peace, processing our trip so far.

In this wide-open space, sound is muffled. The vehicles passing on the highway in the distance are all but noiseless. The only constant is the wind, whipping the energy from inside me, not with velocity but with persistence. Its presence, though distracting, soon becomes companionship, as one realizes it is the only apparent movement in this still land. I can understand how the rocks and mesas have given in to the molding of their forms by the lashing of dirt-laden wind.

Well, they awaken, and we are off, heading for Los Angeles, to pick up the suction dredge.

Fortunately, so far, when one or two people have been out of sorts, someone has remained on an even keel long enough to regain the equilibrium before going off the deep end, leaving the balance to anyone who can cope with it. I pictured, with fear in my heart, the scene when all three of us go off at once. We all seemed to know the limits instinctively. The limits changed with every little nuance of thought, word and deed. Keeping up with the changes was a constant challenge. Three people together is difficult to balance properly.

Sunday, May 18, 1980

Some days are best taken with the grin-and-bear-it approach. Today, I was worn out from the emotional battles with Lee yesterday. I was physically slowed down and overloaded to the point I built an almost touchable wall around myself in my space on the seat of the truck. Last night, after the day of grief, we talked; he continued the tone of the day, saying I had lost my sense of humor. Oh, really? Ha. Ha.

Monday, May 19, 1980

Today we picked up the dredge after spending the night camped out in the parking lot of Keene Engineering. Getting the dredge took several hours since the company did not have our order ready. Actually, they had not even started filling it because they had no record of it. The price of gold is very high right now, causing lots of people to be wanting dredges to cash in on the bonanza. Keene is the only company mass

24

producing gold dredges. They have had more demand than they can keep up with, including their bookkeeping department.

I had the receipt. After getting the paperwork figured out, Keene got our order together piece by piece. I suggested we assemble it in their parking lot but was outvoted by Carole and Lee.

After almost all day, we were loaded up and ready to go. Everybody was mellowed out after two days of tension.

We drove north on Interstate 5 in California, headed toward Sacramento. The 90°F temperature inside the truck cooked us. California's orchards, wheat fields, and vegetable patches flashed past outside the truck window.

May 22, 1980

We crossed over from I-5 to 101, north of Sacramento at Redding. Mt. St. Helens in Washington state had erupted, resulting in I-5 being closed. Fortune was with us. We got to follow the Trinity River, where every few hundred yards, people were dredging for gold. This was the first time Carole and I had seen what we had agreed to do. We took our first pans, across the river from some very paranoid dredgers, some with guns, who seemed overly concerned by our presence. We cut it short out of fear.

After driving north along the coast beginning at Eureka, CA, to somewhere in Oregon, we stopped at a roadside pullout overlooking the ocean. We set up the tent. The beauty of America along with thoughts of the dredges we had seen lightened everyone's hearts.

Lee slept in the truck. In the tent Carole and I got to experience one soggy aspect of camping – wind driven rain. Rainwater blasted through the tent walls and ceiling. We deserved a merit badge or something for getting through that ordeal. I was in shock from the rain coming into the tent as though we did not have a tent. I had expected more from the tent.

When we woke up and dried out, we drove to Astoria, OR, where we were able to drive back over to I-5 which was open again.

Moving north to Seattle, the landscape was changing. The changes in scenery across the country was inspiring. Looking out the window relieved some of the boredom of sitting in the truck day after day.

25

We spent the day in Seattle, looking for a jet unit for the boat motor. Jet units are a replacement for the propeller, allowing boats to drive in shallower water than the usual prop-loaded motor.

A point arrived when Lee wanted to turn back to California and dredge on the Trinity. After I resisted, we decided to go on to Alaska. No going backward. We had plans.

Thursday May 22, 1980

We have momentarily stopped the truck to look at the map, in British Columbia, Canada. We are watching for moose, deer, ducks, and elk, which we have been seeing with frequency. Also, while hanging around outside the truck, we noticed the fresh air which appeared when we left the big cities behind.

What a trip this is. Lee has had some extreme ups and downs. Both he and Carole have drunk enough beer to start a bar. Somehow, we are making it work.

I am the cohesive bond. I am worn out from dealing with these changes. I hope this settles down when we are not cooped up in the truck. Six days so far with at least three more to go. By this time, we have traveled 3,000 miles from Memphis. I feel as though I live in this 3' X 5' space with two roommates. As you know, roommates are not my forte.

How did MIT go? I tried to call you at one point before you were supposed to be gone. Maybe I just thought about it. Days are starting to run together with each one looking a lot like the day before.

We just had a mini confrontation. Carole said that when she gets along with me, she cannot get along with Lee and vice virtue. I know that this will all work out; well, I hope it will! I don't think the tape deck blasting out for six hours has helped my nerves. I turn it down; Carole turns it up. Lee turns it down; she turns it up. These youngsters! These oldsters! And I just broke one of my few remaining fingernails!

I think, providing I live through this and the summer ahead, I will be a hermit for a while. Maybe this is just stir-crazy talk. Changes wear me out.

I wish you were here. Maybe you could give us the benefit of your counsel, though I don't know where you would sit on this truck seat.

I left Walter in my apartment. Last night, I called him and felt a strong desire to go home, where the hassles are more familiar. Plus there

26

is more elbow room! I told him if he wanted to come up to the mining area, he did not need to bring anything but a vacuum cleaner. I guess the homesickness has passed because I am not thinking of vacuum cleaners anymore. Talk of vacuum cleaners shows how much I don't know about where we are going.

Sunday, May 25, 1980
Is it possible that we are finally here? I will put this in the mail tomorrow in Chicken, AK!!!!!!!!

We are camped with several other groups of dredgers a half mile below the South Fork bridge. We are all launching out of this spot and going downriver to whichever areas each group of us has chosen to mine. The tall tales have begun, with all kinds of stories being told. Most frequent topics: gold, bears, guns. I have noticed gold miners are a lot like fishermen. The gold gets bigger with the telling. Pretty much everyone walks around with a gun on their hip or in their hand.

Yesterday, we started putting the dredge together. When we got to the framework, we found that Keene had not put in one nut or bolt, much less the hundred we need to put it together. We had to go to Tok, 100 miles away, to buy them. When we could not find the bolts we needed in Tok, our next move was to drive to Anchorage, 325 miles further, to the Keene dealer where we were told that since we did not buy the dredge from them, they would not supply them for free! We were only too glad to buy them.

I had left my wallet and checkbook back in camp, already used to not needing them for this lifestyle. Thinking we were only going to Tok, I just brought some cash. We found ourselves in a pickle. I thought to call a high school friend I had not talked to in the last 19 years since we graduated and went off to different colleges. He was not at home, but his wife, Trudy, was. I had never met her. I identified myself and told her my story and asked to borrow $40, with a promise to send her a check as soon as I got back to my checkbook. Most people might have hung up. Trudy didn't.

She said, "That is such a wild story. Since my husband is a lawyer, I think you will not try to get away without paying it back. So, yes, I will loan you the money." Thus began one of my longest friendships and a lesson in the Alaskan way of helping each other out.

We bought our supplies and went back to 40 Mile and putting the dredge together.

The day we began our move downriver, Carole and I were on the dredge platform, floating the dredge while Lee drove the boat full of dredge pieces. We had floated about one mile down from the launch point, when the dredge got hung up on the only big rock sticking up out of the river. Lee kept yelling from the boat for one of us to jump in and push it off the rock. Neither one of us wanted to get wet. We said no. He said yes and kept insisting one of us get in the water.

After losing rock, paper, scissors, I got in the river and pushed the dredge off the rock. I had on denim jeans, a fabric that, when wet, gets stiff as a board and takes days to dry. Getting back on the dredge was difficult. The jeans would not bend, a situation that happened two more times in the next few days. That's when I mostly quit wearing jeans and began wearing clothing different from any I had worn in my life: casual and comfortable, more of my transformation to the 40 Mile lifestyle.

One of the skills I am perfecting, is how to pee outside without peeing on my feet. Sounds easy, but there are tricks involved. Most important is standing on an incline, with my bootie facing downhill. One other consideration is the direction the wind is blowing. And third, is anybody watching? Girls must always have toilet paper with them; I have pieces everywhere—to blow my nose on, use at the potty, and to check the oil. Who knew there was so much to this camping thing?

An older woman bulldozer (Caterpillar or Cat) miner from Napoleon Creek and I were hanging out talking at the landing. At some point, she needed to go into the woods to potty. I offered her some of my toilet paper. She said, "No. I use leaves or grass."

Are you kidding me? On the rarest occasions, I have remembered her advice when I needed to, and yes, it does kind of work. I will never use it enough to get proficient!

Well, dear friend, I am done for now.

Take care. From one who is in it up to her ears. Janice

This letter was written to Walter Partridge, soulmate in Memphis, two weeks after we arrived at Chicken, AK:
Friday June 13, 1980

28

Oh, Walter, I have already broken my promise to write every day. Somehow, it did not seem that enough was happening to write about. Today, I realized that small occurrences here are actually the things worth noting.

Looking out the tent door at the river flowing by, beneath this overcast sky, I realize that the scene in front of me is not static but constantly changing. The current and depth of the river are never the same, creating, for those who will notice, variety and comforting sameness from which to take excitement.

Across the river is a cliff with a few spruce, birch, and quaking aspen trees. They, also, are changing all the time with wind blowing their leaves or branches causing different noises and fluttering. The colors over there have gone through several phases already. Imagine what is to come, as summer is just beginning.

In the river, our boat and dredge add some measure of "civilization," though most people probably would not find them enough to replace television and other people.

As we were making pancakes this morning, a loud thrashing of water broke into our microcosm. When we jumped up and out of the tent, we saw a cow moose running upriver through our picture window world. She had been walking in the river quietly enough for us not to have heard her, until she caught our scent and panicked. She showed her fear by running with great strength and much churning of water, incredibly fast, in the two-foot-deep water, demonstrating a reason for those long legs. We know I could not have seen that in Memphis!

Carole left yesterday. Lee would not take her upriver. As luck would have it, some rafters camped across the river from us night before last. It had not happened before and would not happen again. It is remarkable how these guys showed up exactly when they were needed. She grabbed her belongings when Lee was not around, waded across to the rafters' camp, and asked them if she could go with them. Of course, they said yes. It was probably the only time in their lives they would meet a beautiful woman in the woods pretty much in the middle of nowhere, seeking a ride. If she had waited one more day, this would not have happened the way it did, as the river rose a little overnight, so she could not have waded across.

When Lee found out, he went berserk. Surprisingly, he did not take the gun and go to their camp where he was outnumbered. He was not a man who confronted other men. He was a jealous human being, who had worked hard to keep his wished-for harem pitted against each other and felt he had possession of Carole.

We heard later she had hung around Chicken for a few days, got a ride to Fairbanks and caught a plane home to Memphis. At that moment in time, I was wishing I had gone too. I felt I could not go. I owned all that equipment, which was not all paid for, and leaving it would be tantamount to throwing that money away. Now, I am alone with Lee.

A week later, with the water back down, Lee and I attempted to take the boat upriver in an effort to get out to Fairbanks where we had business to attend to. We also wanted to see other miners in other camps. The first two or three miles driving upriver were tiring as we had to keep jumping out to pull the boat through low rapids and high rocks. After an exhausting hour, we turned around and headed home. We figured out that if we had this much trouble this early in the trip, how were we going to get the 19 or so miles up to the truck?

When we had decided to go out, we had to launch our boat, which had been pulled onto dry land, with much effort by Carole, Lee, and me. I could not imagine how Lee and I could pull it back into the water. I should not have worried. Lee is so smart. He located two logs which we put under the boat by tilting up one side of the boat, then the other. With relative ease we rolled the boat into the river.

This was the point I realized how much he knew about the life we were living here. He can drive the boat, take the boat, dredge, and truck motors apart and put them back together in running order, and even cook!!! He can build a campfire with one match and wet wood in the pouring rain (or that is what he says!). He repaired the holes in the boat, maneuvered the 350 pound gas barrels into it, and knew enough physics to enable one man with an injured back and one woman to maneuver that loaded boat into the water. He knows how to dive, a necessity when using this big suction dredge. He can shoot a gun with deadly accuracy, a skill necessary for peace of mind in this bear country.

The river rose about six inches last night, up to the tailing piles where our loose dredge things were. Fortunately, we are learning, little by little, how precious every little wrench and bucket is. Things were picked up and accounted for. Next, maybe we will learn to put them somewhere they will not get wet.

Well, dear friend, I just wanted to let you know what's up around here. Keep the cards and letters coming. Love ya. Janice

This letter was written to Carole two months after we got to the 40 Mile: Tuesday, July 15, 1980

Dear Carole,

I appreciate the letter. I'm glad you are back in Memphis safe and sound and don't have to look for a job until September.

A week or so after you left, an extended rainstorm over the whole 40 Mile area caused the river to rise again. For a day and night, we moved everything up, including the gas barrels. The water finally quit rising at 1 a.m. when it reached the top step you made. I thought we were going to have to move the big tent up to the top of the hill in the middle of the night. The water was lapping at the front door. Two weeks passed before the water went down and cleared up enough so we could dredge again.

We have found that most of the Butte Creek area we are prospecting has been ice drifted, winter work that requires melting the ice in order to mine the bottom of the river. The spot where we were dredging when you were here was the most gold-laden yet. We have spent the last two weeks dredging ground which has already been ice drifted by the old time miners who lived in the two dilapidated cabins on the riverbank. Therefore, we have only found 2.5 ozt since you left. We are usually discouraged beyond description. We have decided to use up the gas we have down here before moving, possibly to the Napoleon Creek area of the river.

Gary and Rich Goodson and Clyde Miles moved down here for two weeks around July 4. The ground they were working here at Butte had been previously worked also, so they moved back up to Uhler Creek, three or four miles upriver. Now, we're alone again. Having company for a while was a treat, even though most of the conversation was gold miner talk. It was weird that they came down and put their dredge right in front of us. We were all out in the middle of nowhere, 13 miles from the nearest mining. Their dredging stirred up the river bottom enough that Lee had trouble seeing underwater. (Years later I learned they had moved down to try to run us off by establishing territorial rights on ground they thought might be rich. At the time, the river was not claimable.)

Lee fixed the air compressor after we got back from Fairbanks and borrowed some weights from another dredger, Mike Dean. Both things made the dredging easier. The motors also now start on the first try. We have the intake pumps sealed, so finally the dredge seems to be in good working order.

We have abundant blueberries right now. Yum. Yum.

The little stink bugs have given way to new and different bothersome bugs. Mosquitoes here are so numerous, you could say they are omnipresent, enough to drive a person insane. Everywhere one looks, there are nine or a thousand or a million of the little suckers. Buzz buzz buzz. If there is one in the tent, I cannot sleep until it is killed. I know that it will bite me if I don't get it first. They are merciless and blood thirsty. One just bit me as I wrote. I read somewhere that only the females bite, needing the blood for the reproductive cycle, but how does one tell which is female and which is male? Their buzzing sounds the same to me. When I am outside panning the concentrates, with both hands occupied, I cannot believe how crazy I feel when hearing the swarms around my ears. I was finally driven to wear the head net, which gave me more or less instantaneous peace of mind. Though they still buzz around, I know they cannot get me. Great invention.

The weather for the last three days has been a pleasant 75°F. Considering the news about record setting heat in the South, I feel very lucky to be here.

So far, we have had no more bear visitations. (More on this later.)

My hands are a wreck. First to bite the dust was my right index finger. The fingernail was lost to a rivet hole in the boat, while trying to be the little Dutch boy whose finger in the dike saved the whole town from drowning. We had just driven over a big, bad rock sticking up out of the water, tearing out the rivet and making our first hole in the boat. Lee told me to put my finger on the resulting hole to keep water from coming into the boat. There was a bracket over the space where my finger and the hole were. Wouldn't you know it, we hit another rock! The bottom of the boat flexed upward and squeezed my finger between the bottom of the boat and the bracket, making a three-quarter impression of the rivet. Blood went everywhere. Not being much of an outdoors person yet, I thought it was worse than it turned out to be. I now have a rivet impression on one side of my finger and a fingernail resembling Aurora Borealis in blue, brown, and pink, on the other.

Next came the great 55-gallon-barrel-over-the-left-hand caper. Lee was in the bed of the truck, which was parked on an incline down to the river at the landing. He was preparing to roll off a full barrel weighing around 350 pounds to get it from the truck over to the boat.

He suggested, "Stop this barrel from rolling into the river. Don't let it get started down the hill. You will not be able to stop it."

Of course, there was no way I was able to perform this maneuver. This one elicited screaming from me, as I heard or felt, I'm not sure which, the pop, pop, pop of three of my knuckles as the barrel rolled over my hand, pushing it back toward my arm. I was positive my hand and wrist were smashed. After the dust settled and the chips were in, my hand was swollen and very colorful as the bruises healed, with various sprains and broken blood vessels. You can tell by these descriptions that I was beginning to make a fine display canvas for showy hues, tinges, and tones.

Since the preceding, nothing major has happened. Minor things added up to many gashes, cuts, abrasions, and contusions. I had bruises from ankle to hip and injuries to all but two fingers. Those healthy fingers' days are numbered if experience is taken into consideration. I began to realize if things did not change, there would not be enough left of me to gather together to go home at the end of the season.

Hard, hard work with all manner of problems. Rocks stop up the hose or venturi area of the jet tube, where the jet and pump hoses come together. Moving the dredge from place to place would be hard enough. In our case, we have different pontoons from other dredges. They are usually full of water, adding tremendous weight. We are often draining our leaky pontoons to be sure they float well enough to maintain the correct angle of the sluice box. The diver and the dredge fight the current. The weather makes a tough job tougher. Being a gofer, raking rocks, picking up the nozzle in hip-deep water, cooking, cleaning, etc., wears me out. I cannot even read, much less write.

Today, we wanted to move the dredge forward, but due to the current, the water-filled pontoons, and our discouragement arising from finding very little gold, we finally quit for the day, angry at each other. Our frustration arose out of the situation, not out of dissatisfaction with each other. Walking back to the camp along the sandy beach, full of woe, I was filled with wonder, as eight purple butterflies fluttered around my feet. Somehow, I was right with the world again, even though the work problems had not corrected themselves and will have to be faced tomorrow.

I have a "gold is everywhere" continuing saga. Now, in addition to being in the drinking water, between the rocks, and in our gold jars, it is in the sand caught on my socks by my sandals. (Looking back, I know this "gold" must have been fool's gold of some kind, mica probably.)

I have many thoughts in my mind about Memphis. I dream a lot about people there. Overall, though, I think I have made the adjustment to this place and lifestyle. And what an adjustment it is! I find myself dreaming of steak, ice cream and salad bars too!

Last week, I got a month's worth of mail, eight or nine letters. What a treat! I've read them over and over. The news never seems to get stale. Maik Schluroff says he wishes he was here. If he only knew!

Recently, I drank a quart of milk at one time. The next day my sinuses were stopped up. My face looked like a balloon. I was hoping I did not die of a brain infection. I wonder if your sinus condition is related to milk consumption also.

I miss you a bunch. Janice

After I wrote these letters, Lee mostly quit dredging, preferring instead to be in the boat going to the Napoleon camp, where he drove himself crazy with jealousy protecting me from any and all contact with anything male. In a camp with 14 guys and one woman, he was kept busy. Simultaneously he attempted to coerce any drugs or alcohol he could get from any source.

One time he scraped a mattress, hoping to round up something to get high with. I realized by that time what a mess I was in, but being the owner of all that heavy equipment tied me to it. When he told me he was going up to the landing to get in the truck and drive 260 miles to go fishing, there was not much that I could do. My choices were staying alone in camp for who knew how long or go too. If I was with him, I could encourage him to get back to business.

There came a time when he hit me while we were dredging. I think it was in the middle of the summer. I did not quite have my skills honed at that point, so I stayed, marking my time until I could make that right.

The next time we went up to Napoleon, I told my buddies Ross Davis and Mud Sweeten. They took him into the woods and gave him some mind-adjusting therapy.

He did not ever hit me again. I knew I could not trust him not to go off the deep end though. This added another layer of anxiety to the lack of gold and the general slacking off, in the quickly approaching end of the season with very little money to pay my bills. Lee did not have to worry about it because he did not have any money invested in anything and did not need any money. He would be just as happy sleeping in the truck all winter as not.

I will say he taught me some of what is important in life. All a person really needs is food, warmth, and a few basics. In this society, we are bombarded with advertisements making us think a lot of things are necessities that turn out not to be.

I underwent a transition in my soul that summer from accumulating to divesting. My life was lightened up as far as possessions were concerned, except for the dredge and other equipment, objects of great value out here, which now held me prisoner. And, I still had to pay those bills.

Lee was my partner for the first year.

6. SUCTION DREDGE

The diver is the hump in the river in front of the dredge. Showing the full processing mode, the turbulence in the sluice box contains the overburden the diver is sucking up. The gold is supposed to fall out in the front of the box. This is what we live for. Our biggest hope right this minute is that the material being sucked up is full of gold! We are always glad when the dredging is going smoothly.

What is a suction dredge?

Basically, it is a motorized, floating sluice box. A gas engine runs a water pump, which creates suction in a hose. This results in an action like a very powerful vacuum cleaner, sucking up the loose material in its path underwater. This material, called overburden, contains gravel, black sand, garnets, hematite, and gold, for example. The material sometimes includes bedrock, the usually solid rock that underlies the loose material, depending on the conditions in the river bottom. It is combined with river water, which is sucked up at the same time.

All of it is carried up the hose and into the diffuser. Here, it combines with water from the water pump under high flow and decreased pressure coming in through the venturi, a tube or tubes welded to a hole in the diffuser which contains water being pumped into the system by a water pump. This combination results in a slowing down and spreading out of the material in the water in the diffuser.

The whole mixture is blasted at a prescribed rate over the sluice box. Ideally, the heavier material, including gold, which is one of the heaviest constituents of river gravel, has settled in the diffuser before it gets to the sluice box. The heaviest material drops into the first few feet of the box, while the lighter is flushed off the end. Simple as that.

This results in a self-reclaiming process, whereby everything but the heaviest, gold-bearing component goes off the end of the sluice and fills up the hole that the front of the dredge is making.

All of this is floating in water, which in our case, was the 40 Mile River. When we were finished at the end of the season, only a hole the size of the dredge remained to indicate that we were ever there. Flooding, which occurs after spring thaw or heavy rains, fills in the hole as rocks shift around on the river bottom.

This is the hole made with the suction hose. The rocks piled around inside the hole were moved by hand by the diver because they were too large to go up the 8" hose. Photo by James Putman.

There are many sizes of dredges. Most dredgers have more than one size for different uses. Almost all dredges require a diver in the water to guide the nozzle through the process. At the same time the diver is moving rocks larger than the hose diameter by hand, out of the way, so they will not get stuck in the hose or on the front of the nozzle.

Divers also have a blaster fastened to the suction hose. The blaster works like a garden hose with a sprayer. The diver can use the blaster to dislodge compacted areas with a stream of water under pressure, which would take a long time if worked by hose alone.

As I finish this book after all these years, things have changed again on the river. Dredgers are now using little excavators to load their sluice boxes. I don't know how much diving is involved.

The big modern portable dredges, 6" and larger, the name coming from the diameter of the suction hose, involve a diver being underwater. The diver wears a wetsuit, face mask and regulator, and gets his/her air from an air compressor on the dredge platform.

In these Alaskan waters, we also pumped hot water to the diver. We heated it by wrapping copper tubing through which cold water flowed, around the exhaust pipe on the engine. We attached a long, flexible water hose to the copper tube. The hose was fitted with a valve

Roger Tallini, suited up, testing the temperature of the water coming out of the tube before he puts the tube into his suit. This water will keep him warm while he is underwater no matter what the temperature of the river water is. He is standing on a Precision 8" dredge. To protect his suit's legs while he is on his knees working, he is wearing inner tube sections over his legs.

for adjusting the temperature, then inserted into the diver's suit. In this way, the diver could be comfortable for extended periods of time in cold river water. It was like being in a bathtub full of warm water.

The angle of the sluice box in relation to the diffuser – the metal tube between the hose and sluice box where water and material mix and begin the processing – is critical, as is the setup of the box.

We (me and my partners over the years) were always changing around the hardware in the box to maximize the capturing of the gold in the sluice. Some of the hardware included the riffles – baffle-like obstructions, expanded metal, and punch plate. All of the hardware gave the gold a protected place to settle. We had two or three different kinds of carpet, as well as an ever-changing combination of heavy metal in the box, all to capture every little speck of gold.

All miners had ideas about how best to set up the box. It was always a topic of discussion and hot debate. We tried almost anything.

We had a saying: "The pay is in the fines." Since 99% of all the gold that has ever been found is fine gold, we had to respect each small piece that came across the sluice box.

The nuggets, comprising the other 1%, were few and far between, so our box was set up for fine gold recovery. If we happened to get into a nugget patch, we would stop and change the box to capture the larger-sized gold. Although this was a rare occurrence, the diver was aware of it immediately since the nuggets could be seen underwater.

In our case, we saved every nugget we found over the years and lived off the proceeds of the fines.

At the end of every dredging day, we would clean up the front four feet of the box where most of the gold was located. We left the back eight feet of the 12-foot box until we were able to pan gold from the back riffles, meaning that the back of the box was getting loaded up with gold or that the gold was being flushed back and likely out of the box for some reason.

We would take occasional pans from various places in the box, but we paid particular attention to the last 12 inches of the box. When we found anything in the pan, we would do a whole box cleanup. This process took up to two days and usually yielded only a small percentage when compared to the fronts that we cleaned up every day. Still, every little bit added up. We were vigilant about this. Dredging up the gold was hard work. We did not want it going off the end of the box back into the river.

Cleaning the first four feet took a total of about six hours, so the job was usually split up by camp members. The front of the box was more likely to have nuggets which fall out first.

Nuggets are rare, resulting in higher prices per unit than the fines. A one-ounce nugget is rarer than a 5-carat diamond, while fines are valued at a percentage of the spot price based on their assay. This is because they are common, comprising 99% of all gold.

Even the smallest pieces of gold dust have astonishing weight. The weight can be heard by dropping one flake onto a piece of paper where it makes a clunking sound, much louder than it seemingly should.

We cleaned the first four feet by lifting metal riffles off the carpet lining the bottom of the box. Then we dunked the carpet to clean the concentrates out in a 32-gallon plastic garbage can full of water used as a mining tool. The concentrates fell to the bottom of the garbage can. After pouring off most of the water so we could lift it, we took our garbage can home to finish the processing.

Every step in the cleanup takes the gold closer to a gravel free state, just gold flakes or dust or nuggets. Therefore, each step magnifies any mistake because anything that gets lost is more likely to be gold in the later stages of the cleanup.

After spending nine hours dredging, then adding on six hours for cleaning all the way to being in the bottle, even when sharing the daily cleanup duties, our days were long. We also had cooking, resting, getting wood for the wood stove, and other camp chores.

When I was the camp person and not working on the dredge, which happened when Kurt worked with us or when we camped with the other guys, I did almost all the gathering, transporting, and cutting of the wood. This allowed the divers to be warm without energy draining camp work. I did the cooking and finished cleaning gold.

Our whole focus was on dredging. Gold could always be cleaned on flood days, but dredging had to be done whenever it could be done. In fact, probably the biggest key to our success was prioritizing making the most of the short Alaskan mining seasons. For three or four months every year, our focus was on finding and capturing the gold in the water. We missed many 4th of July picnics and visits with people boating by because we kept dredging when we could.

When we first began dredging, cleanup at our camp was done by panning six hours a day. However, this changed at the beginning of the third year. Then, we got a gold wheel, a spinning wheel with spiral leads and spray bar that automatically separated the gold from the lighter black sand. This wheel was a great invention, one I appreciated from the first use. It cost $500, a bargain after all the hours we had spent panning down concentrates over the years.

Gold being separated from the black sand. Gold is going up the spiral and through the hole into a bucket. Black sand, being lighter, is washed down and off the lip of the wheel and into the tub below to be thrown back in front of the dredge so we could suck up any gold that got past these efforts to capture it.

Although we still had to pan down gold larger than the window screen we used as a classifier to make the fines all one size, we could wheel down the fines in 30 minutes. Panning had taken us many hours in past years.

The wheel was run by a 12V battery and a windshield washer motor, a combination that was very dependable. We almost never had trouble with breakdowns of the gold wheel.

These pictures show three different cleanup methods. There are many more, including panning the concentrates down.

What made all of this gold mining function was the fact that most of the gold on the 40 Mile is placer gold. This means it is loose in the gravel, unlike lode gold which is locked in rock that has to be crushed in order to separate the gold.

A gold pan, sluicing, high banking, suction dredging, Cat mining, and hydraulicking are forms of placer mining.

Another method of cleanup was using a sluice inside the empty sluice box on the dredge, an easy place to set it up. This sluice has fine gold in it.

Miller Table: Another cleanup tool uses a thin film of water dripping over a sloping slate table. Water dripping out of orange distributor tube floats black sand off table leaving gold behind. The operator is Roger Tallini.

7. DIVERS AND DREDGERS

When I first started mining with Lee, I tried to work the nozzle of the 8″ dredge, which is dredging lingo for being under water guiding the hose. After getting one hand sucked into the nozzle and not being able to get it out, then getting a foot sucked into the nozzle and not being able to get it out, I did not try again. We had to turn the dredge off to stop the suction when I got body parts sucked up.

The dredging job of tender, the person who works on the deck of the bigger dredges, which I did, consists of, among other things: Watching the diver's bubbles to check that he hasn't been killed by a rock he has dislodged, moving piles of tailings when necessary, loosening and tightening ropes to position the dredge, and using the ram rod to try to loosen rocks stuck in the hose. Stuck rocks can involve enormous amounts of time and generate much frustration for both the diver and the tender. It is often an intense workout. One of the questions that arises surrounding this situation is: How can one rock get so stuck?

I also filled the gas tanks of the dredge engines and watched the time which is very important to the person under the water.

I moved lots of rocks by hand in my day while tending. When the river water level was down, the tailings got stuck in the sluice box or piled up around the end of the box. They had to be moved by hand. To give the reader something to relate to: Have you ever moved a pile of rocks from here to over there? Since it is part of dredging, we did it often.

In those days, there weren't many 6″ dredges. People had 5″ or 8″ dredges. The 5″ is not able, by far, to move as much ground as the 8″, which is a hog and really needs two people working it, one on top and one underwater. The 6″ has turned out to be ideal in a lot of places for one person to work comfortably and profitably. Having a 6″ earlier in my career might have changed some things, as it did in my later years.

When everything is working smoothly, leaning into the ultra-serene environment is very Zen. When things aren't working smoothly, not so Zen. All of the tasks I did could be done by the divers. Since they did not have to do them when I did them, I saved their energy, allowing them to dive more.

I want to emphasize how rare being a woman in a dredge camp or working on a dredge is. There were a few women divers over the years. Laura dove for Kurt and me for a short time. Jan Flora had a 4″ or 5″ dredge she used on her own claim for several years. And these days, Dawn Reeves suits up and works alongside her husband, Chuck. So, it has been and continues to be done.

I owned a complete dredge operation. I worked on the dredge. I did not dive. I was in some limbo place between being fully a dredger and not, while being fully committed to the whole experience. The short answer to all this doubt is that dredging is teamwork. We were a team.

Several wives spent summers on the river. Eva Scofield worked with her husband Pat, during the years they dredged the 40 Mile. JoAnn Weber, their daughter, also spent summers out there, while her partner Randy Raffety worked on the dredge with Pat. Sharon and Bryon Young worked together, as did Don and Jane Hart. Linda and Wayne Duke were a dredging team for a while. Barbara and Rod Knight, sourdoughs in the best sense of the word, spent many summers dredging and raising a family on the banks of the river. Though few are far between, these women were committed to the dredging lifestyle.

Outsiders might not understand the reasons for our living in tents and other imagined deprivations. No wonder we women were glad to see each other on the rare occasions we crossed paths. We were understood.

Recently, a guy mining friend told me I was not a dredger. I was shocked into uncertainty. Having been totally committed to the profession in all the other ways, I examined my validity. My conclusion is that I am a woman dredger but not a diver. Again, we were a team. I owned the dredge, which is more than a lot of men divers can say, owned claims and was out there 16 years working on the river. What more does it take?

Roger Tallini Discusses the Diver's Point of View

Being a dredger in Alaska is no easy task and it has broken the spirit of many a person who believed they could handle it.

You must wrestle with a 10–15-foot stiff hose with a 30-pound nozzle at the end of it for your entire 2–3 hour dive. If you're using an 8″ dredge nozzle with a 7″ sizing ring, all rocks over 7″ must be lifted and moved aside. If it's a 10" dredge nozzle with a 9" sizing ring, all rocks over 9" must be moved aside.

The river's current is always against you, restricting your motion, causing you to lean into it. You are always fighting it until you can hide behind your cut, which is the wall that forms as the hole gets deeper.

The wet suit adds a lot of buoyancy to a diver, and in order for him to stay on the bottom of the river, he must wear a weight belt. The depth of the water and the force of the current dictates the amount of weight to be used. When dredging toward the middle of the river 60-90 pounds of weight may be necessary, while dredging close to shore only 15-30 pounds may be needed.

In the 40 Mile, the water is tea colored, which adds a dimension of darkness when the diver is underwater. During high water times when the water gets muddy, visibility can drop to near zero. All divers set their own limits for days they will dive when the water is muddy. Some must see their hand when outstretched at arm's length; others may only need a foot of visibility. During muddy days, being underwater can be claustrophobic; you don't know where you are or what's happening around you. It's not for the faint of heart.

So, picture a person with 60 pounds of weight around his waist, on the bottom of a muddy river, in fast moving current, constantly moving up and down a 30-pound nozzle with an equally heavy and awkward hose attached, sucking up rocks. All the while you are dredging, you are moving oversized rocks out of the way or prying loose oversized rocks that are stuck in the nozzle. Couple all this with rocks that get clogged in the hose that must be beat loose and dealing with smashed hands and fingers from the rocks.

You would have to say, there must be an easier way to make a living…why would anyone want to put up with all this?

There are those times, however, when the water is at its clearest and the sun is shining through the water, that the beauty of being underwater takes hold of you, like when the grayling fish come into your cut, swim around you and greet you as one of their own and the glitter of yellow gold pours off your cut and into your nozzle.

Those days are the ones I remember most. The ones that override the smashed fingers, the struggle and the exhaustion. The days of peace and joy of finding God's treasure in this remote land.

Roger's diving perspective shows what being underwater was all about. It also accurately describes why I couldn't do it with the dredge I had (too big) and why I fall into some subset category in the dredging community.

My not diving made it less productive because with two divers more gold can be produced. We discovered over time that more is only one way to look at it. But dredging is body thrashing work. There is much to be said for having help and slowing physical breakdown by spreading out the diving work. However, with additional divers, more claims are needed because the ground is sucked up faster. Life becomes more complicated.

8. SOME INFORMATION ABOUT THE GOLD

A dredger taking a sample to pan. This is one type of prospecting.
This could be the next hot spot. 40 Mile River water has tannin in it,
making the water tea color.

How did we turn the fine gold into money? We took it to a refiner/assayer who gave us the spot price of gold minus the assay. For example, if gold was $1000/ozt and our gold assayed 85% gold, our beginning total for an ounce was $1000/ozt x 0.85 = $850. Some refiners gave us the silver content which in our case was about 12% of the total.

Before we got the check, certain fees were subtracted. First was the melt loss fee, a charge of usually 2% or 3%. Then, the assay fee, the process that determines how much of the sample is gold, which in our case was from 80% to 85%. And last was the refiner's fee of $125. We felt lucky to come away with 80%.

Nuggets sell for more because they are rare and can be sold online at auction sites like eBay for a premium or at the refiner for at least spot price. The increased value over fines is due to their rarity, not their assay.

Sometimes I see fines packaged up and being sold on eBay at a slightly higher price than the refiner. Going to the refiner is easier which sometimes counts. Especially when larger amounts are being sold.

Roger Tallini holding a weighing tray containing 140 ozt of his fine gold. No wonder he is smiling.

During our mining span, the price of gold went from about $128/ozt to $2025/ozt today. Most of the time that we dredged, gold was $300 to $500 an ounce.

Early 1977 saw the price at $128/ozt. By year's end the price was up to $170/ozt. By 1980 the price started the year at about $480 and seesawed to $760 by late September. After falling through all of 1981, gold price found itself at $410.

Most of the years we were dredging, gold was between $300 and $500, give or take. Then again, that was long ago when $300 was worth more than $300 is today.

As a matter fact. if Lee and I had sold one ounce in September at $760 when we came off the river, the spot price by today's price would have been $2829.21! This represents an increased value of 3.72 times spot price from 1980 to 2024.

9. SEASON'S END OR MORE OF THE SAME

When Lee and I went anywhere in the boat, upon arrival he would say, "Jump out and tie off the boat." I would get out on the side and immediately take a bath in the river, swept off my feet by the current, getting wet even if I had stayed dry during the whole trip up to this point. I noticed this happened to no one else. I asked him why. He said to try getting off the front of the boat. When I asked him if he was ever going to tell me that, he said probably not. I found that funny, in truth. He was teaching me things I would need to know in this new world I was in. And guess what? I stopped getting wet that way! Still, it showed something not necessarily good about Lee.

After snow fell Labor Day night (September 1, 1980), I began to lose my ability to cope with Butte Creek. When I awoke that morning, I could tell something was different about the day. As I looked up at the top of my tent from inside my sleeping bag, I thought Lee had thrown a tarp over it because the tent inside was darker than usual. When I opened the door, the world was white! Snow falls softly; I had not been aware it was happening. Four inches had fallen that night, which melted as the day went on. The arrival of the snow, when added to the rest of our challenging existence, was more than I could handle. I could not summon my usual Pollyanna optimism.

Sometime during this period, the boat motor quit working, leaving us stranded nine miles from the nearest humans. We both saw it as an opportunity to do some uninterrupted dredging, but the river was muddy every day from sunup until sundown.

A Cat miner upriver had been sluicing illegally all summer, without settling ponds, muddying the river below him, including our part. Several of the dredgers had talked to him and tried to schedule times for his sluicing that would not mud us out. However, since the dredgers were strung out for many miles along the river, finding a time that worked for all of us was not possible.

The Cat miner did not care about us anyway. He continued sluicing without ponds whenever he felt like it. I heard through the grapevine that somebody put sugar in his gas tanks one night to shut him down. Maybe it was just wishful thinking. If it was done, it did not slow him down.

The time or two we attempted to dredge in the muddy water, Lee could not see underwater, making it more possible for a mishap, such as a big rock falling onto his head or air hose. Falling rocks came out of the wall of the hole he made as he worked the ground. These rocks could be seen when the water was clear. Other factors, such as 38°F water in the days before hot water in the suits and priming on freezing days for an hour to thaw all the frozen parts and getting the dredge started, took away any remaining enthusiasm.

For two or three weeks, the weather was relentlessly chilly. As we waited for the clear, warm fall Indian summer weather we had been led to believe was surely coming, I became more disheartened in 40°F days and 10°F nights. We did not have a wood burning stove or a light. When the sun went down at 6 p.m., we did too if we did not want to sit around outside by the fire pit in the dark.

Finally, we decided to float out because going upriver without a motor wasn't an option. Each passing day under these conditions caused us to feel more hopeless and helpless. We were downriver from everyone else on the South Fork. No potential help boated past our camp. We were on our own, and the winter was fast approaching.

Floating the motorless boat 25 miles downriver to the 40 Mile bridge took us two days. Once there, we found ourselves trying to hitch a ride in the now-falling rain to our truck at South Fork, 38 miles away. After four hours and only three cars driving past our outstretched thumbs, we were despondent. Luckily, Susie McCall from Chicken Bar came by and gave Lee a ride, leaving me to watch the boat and the motor inside the boat, with the Marlin 45-70 for protection.

As darkness fell, I realized that the bears I imagined all around could see me huddled around the fire better than I could see them. Frightened by my thoughts, every minute seemed like eternity!

By the time Lee returned with two guys from South Fork, I was a nervous wreck. The fire had long since gone out. Cold and dark had set in. This area had been camped in for so many years, there was no easily available wood to keep the fire going. We loaded the 450-pound boat, the 240-pound motor, and our gear in the dark.

We spent the night at Phil Schmidt's in South Fork bridge area, after having the truck battery go dead due to a faulty alternator. Using headlights to get back was a necessity due to the dark and yes, fog which had rolled in, adding its two cents' worth.

The half mile drive from the landing down to Phil's camp was one of the scariest rides ever for me. Mud was so deep that the truck with the boat on top of the rack swayed from side to side, as the spinning tires tried to find traction in the soupy mess.

During this slipping and sliding, one of the 55-gallon barrels standing against the back window in the bed of the truck and not tied down, crashed into the window. The window shattered sending thousands of little squares of tempered safety glass flying all over the inside of the truck. Years later, I occasionally find a small square piece of window glass in the truck.

Rain fell all night and during the next day. When we left to go to Chicken to see about the boat motor, the road was worse than the day before. In the middle of our journey, we got a flat tire. Of course, we did not have a spare. Luckily, we did have split rim tires and the tools to break down the tires and repair them. At some point, sheer will to live kicks in. This was one of those times.

These trucks got stuck in the muck 80 years ago and are still stuck today! Just joking, but this muck looks similar to the muck I am talking about. Photo from Mukluk Land, Tok, AK.

The man we hoped would help with the motor was at the Chicken bar drunk and belligerent. We went back to Phil's, down that scary road again, to await the next day when we planned to catch the man before he got drunk.

Next morning, more rain. Slipping and sliding more than ever on the road down to Phil's scared Lee into saying perhaps he should have parked at the landing. This had my full agreement, as my hands held the door armrest for dear life. I resolved not to make that trip in the truck again. Walking that half a mile in the muck was preferable.

Lee did not want to deal with the drunk, so we made two trips in opposite directions on the slippery dirt highway, trying to find someone to help us, as we talked about our situation. We decided to drop the boat off at the landing and drive 100 miles to Tok with the motor, hoping to find someone to help us there.

On the way to the landing to unload the boat, we ran into Ross Davis and Mud Sweeten, the friends who had been like family to me during the summer. The preceding two days had been too much strain. When they offered their boat to us so we could go down to Butte, get my things, and check on the dredge and other things threatened by the rising water, I began crying almost immediately, releasing the tension. We took their offer before they could change their minds.

Back at Butte, our gear was still safe. It was a good thing we returned when we did. With the water coming up close to the lowest level of our camp, we would have lost necessary items if we had not gone back down there when we did. We closed the camp, pulled the dredge up high on the riverbank using the come-along, and took out as much stuff as we could. Dredging would have to continue another year.

Cold temperatures, rain, mal- or non-functioning equipment had taken their toll. I was ready to leave. Besides, the sandhill cranes and Canada geese were flying south, a sure sign it was time to start wrapping it up.

The lifestyle that summer did not lend itself to writing letters, so I fell out of touch with the outside world. Strangely enough, this did not seem to matter. There was really no way to explain what went on out there to someone living in Midtown Memphis.

I had experienced many new things unrelated to anything I had ever done. I gained self-sufficiency I did not know I was lacking. I learned lots that I did not know, especially what is necessary in life on a basic level and the difference between a box open wrench and pliers.

I flew to my mother's in Spokane, WA, leaving Lee in Alaska for the winter.

After visiting a few weeks, I took a Greyhound bus across the top of the country to Memphis. This turned out to be a new kind of trip. The land was different from any I had ever seen.

I wrote in my journal:

Oct 7, 1980: On the express bus, heading east out of Livingston, Montana, my eyes attempt to see into the Yellowstone River valley and surrounding mountains. I'm wondering whether there is any gold in this country.

My mind jumps from gold to Lee and the whole 40 Mile experience, to Spokane, to this bus, and on toward Memphis and Carole and a job. Five months away have left me detached and unable to recall exactly what keeps me in Memphis.

I'm awestruck as usual by this land of ours and excited as we traverse plains and mountains I've never seen before. North Dakota, Minnesota, and Wisconsin are ahead!

Twelve hours down. Only 48 to go! Then, I am home again, back where I started five months before. Inside, though, I am a changed person.

Autumn all around. Oh, so beautiful.

Thirty miles from Billings going east toward Miles City. We're an hour late because the air conditioning was not working. Well, it still isn't. Mesas all around. A black bird with white stripes on its wings and tail just flew by overhead.

Miles City, in Custer County, the heart of range country (as in "Home, home on the..."), has a 4:15 p.m. temperature of 92°F on October 7, and is home of Little Big Men Pizza and other historical reminders.

This land, which looks so monochromatic at first glance, when taken plant by scraggly-looking plant, shouts with variety of texture and color.

We've been following the Yellowstone River valley since Livingston. As miles passed, the mountains along the valley dwindled to mesas, and now, so little remains, I wonder whether this can still be called a valley.

Glendive area: Flat with little bumps. Strange looking country. Mostly, no trees; occasional clusters of deciduous bushes near water.

Just outside and east of Glendive, a drastic change of scenery. Very bumpy, pointed hills with many different colored strata exposed. Many pink tops. (End of journal.)

Some thoughts from the trip:

All this sightseeing would not have been possible from an airplane. However, as night rolled in, I missed vast portions of landscape due to the darkness, and I was still in a bus. We rolled into Fargo, ND, at 2 a.m. Streetlights made it look like so many other places, which was a comfort.

One night, we stopped at a bowling alley at 3 a.m. somewhere isolated, picking up and unloading passengers and getting something to eat. Walking around loose and free for a while rejuvenated the spirit. As we reboarded, the bus driver told me I was cute. Thanks, dude.

We went through Minneapolis/St. Paul during the daylight. And Wisconsin. As the sun was setting, during rush hour, we arrived in Chicago. After changing buses, we headed south in the dark. By the next day, I was back in Memphis with a strong desire to skip the bus riding again for a long time. I would not have missed it for the world this time though.

10. Intervening Year 1981

When I found a job in Memphis in October 1980, the interviewer told me he would not hire me unless I promised not to leave the following spring to go back to the mining. I easily promised I wouldn't. I was so over dredging, I did not think I would ever want to go back.

Lo and behold, the next spring found me knowing I had to go check on my equipment. I had heard that Lee had gone back to the river and had taken over my dredge and boat. I decided I needed to check in with him in person and make some arrangements concerning the storage and possession of the equipment before the season ended, before he just walked away, leaving it for scrounging. 1981 was also my 20th high school reunion in Anchorage.

When I asked for the time off, the boss said I could have one weekend off for the reunion. At that time, I was working all 40 of my weekly hours starting at 3 p.m. on Friday and finishing up at 7 a.m. on Monday, with just enough time off during those workdays to sleep.

Monday came. I got on a plane headed for Anchorage and the reunion. We finished by the following Sunday night. I knew I had to go to 40 Mile even though I had not been given the time off. I took a bus to Tok, the last town before getting out into gold country. At the last pay phone, I made a long-distance call to my friend, Peggy, a nurse in Memphis. We planned that she would call in sick for me on Friday and tell the person who answered the phone that she was taking me to the emergency room because I was sick and probably would not be at work all weekend. She timed it so that the person I would have been working with was the only person there to answer the call. He was often inebriated on the job, which I thought might make him unsure of the facts.

I spent most of the next two weeks hanging out on the 40 Mile in vacation mode with Ross and his crew camped at Napoleon. Lee was dredging two claims down. I got to surprise him by walking into his camp unexpectedly.

We worked out our agreement for the end of the season. He agreed to turn over everything to Ross and walk away. He did ask for the truck, but why, I don't know. At the very time we were talking, he was hiding some relevant information. The boat engine had a blown head, rendering it out of action. The boat itself had many holes and wasn't floating. A few dredge malfunctions had put the dredge out of commission, so he wasn't even dredging. He was on a summer vacation pretending to dredge. Oh well. I had done what I could do for now.

My brother Kurt had tried working with Lee for a short time that summer. When Kurt was underwater, Lee lied about the time Kurt spent sucking up the pay. Lee was the timekeeper and had Kurt doing twice the underwater time. Kurt left because Lee was willing to try to make more while doing less.

I got back to Memphis Thursday night in time to be at work on Friday and never told anyone I worked with what I had been up to. Oh yes, they asked. I did not tell them that I had called in sick from Bush Alaska. I was a conscientious worker after that, trying to make up for what I knew I had burdened my coworkers with.

That winter I took Small Engine Repair, a continuing education course at Memphis State University. The more I could contribute to the river lifestyle, the less I would have to rely on people like Lee, who was not as motivated as I was.

Lee fell asleep at the wheel. The truck was hardly scratched, but Kurt, the passenger, saw his life pass before his eyes.

11. THE SURPRISE ATTACK

Kurt and I decided to join forces and run the dredge together.

We flew to Anchorage on May 12, 1982, with the idea of picking up the truck from Ross, fixing the boat motor which had thrown a rod under Lee's abuse, buying groceries, then getting out to the river ASAP.

We left Anchorage a month later, having done extensive work on the truck: new steering column, brake work, a u-joint, lube job, power steering leak, and a new salvage yard engine.

The engine in the truck was smoking through the heads. When we took off the covers, we found scored valves. When we took off the heads to take them for machine work, we found burned pistons and bent camshaft. In other words, the engine was trashed to its core. That is what happens when it doesn't get oil.

Lee, who had used the truck for two summers, was not one to do maintenance, such as checking the oil, so he had burned up the engine. He was able to repair it. He was not inclined to. If I am honest, the truck was in pretty much the same shape it had been in when Lee found it in that pasture in Tennessee two years before! Kurt, Ross, and I restored it back to glorious life, as we had no vo-tech school to call on this time.

On June 16, Kurt and I finally arrived at Napoleon Creek, where we were going to be mining in the river. Ross had taken possession of the equipment from Lee the previous autumn, storing most of it on the riverbank for the winter.

We found that some of our equipment had been pilfered by people who got there before we did. One item taken was a $6 gas cap for the jet foot. Without the gas cap, the dredge would not run. We had to go to Tok for the replacement cap, a 200-mile round trip. We also had to go 10 miles downriver to rescue the stolen $400 dry suit from a guy, after others at Napoleon ratted him out. His excuse was that we weren't there, so our stuff must be salvage.

Once we got our equipment back, we were up and running. At that time we crossed paths with and hired Laura, a diver, to work on the dredge. This was an unbelievable occurrence. There were not many women divers because most women are not strong enough to handle an 8" dredge. Our partnership lasted a week until Laura went to Chicken to check her mail and did not return. Thank goodness for the gossip mill around the mining area. We learned the troopers were at the post office looking for her for selling land she did not own in Washington state. They arrested her and took her away.

On July 16, Mom came for a visit. At the time, she was 59 years old and quite adventurous which was a good thing because setup did not go smoothly with the dredging or the boat. We did not get the kinks worked out until after her visit.

On Sunday July 24, a helicopter landed on the gravel bar outside our kitchen tent. Two troopers climbed out. Brenda Bass, our next-door neighbor, Shasta, her apricot toy poodle, Mom, and I went down to greet them. The troopers carried a pile of summons for a few of the more well-known miners and Jane Doe #1-#30 and John Doe #1-#30 for the unknown miners. There was one for everybody!

We talked a while. The upshot was that the infamous Russells, who had not been around for three years, were now using a false name and were suing everybody to get 10 percent of the gold found on the claim. They also wanted to get us off the claim where our camp was and to take away our equipment and our vehicles. To fight this land and property grab, we had to be in court on Thursday in Fairbanks, 300 miles from where we were standing!

The Russells were former Cat miners up Napoleon Creek who owned land claims on both sides of the river and had decided they wanted a piece of the frenzied action in the river bottom. They were going to court to kick us off the river bottom claims, which were not part of their claims.

Brenda, Shasta, Mom, and I said goodbye to the troopers. Then, one of them said thanks for not shooting them! What? They said we had the reputation of being the bad Napoleon Creek gang. Ha. We weren't even carrying guns. I said, "If it will make you feel any better, I will run up and get a gun!" One of the troopers said if we shot them, there would be five more to take their place. Brenda said we could use the company. Dangerous conversation.

The Russells had lived up Napoleon Creek, during the 1970s, with two from their camp being involved in the shooting deaths, on the frozen river, of two other miners December 22, 1977. One of those two troublemakers was later involved in the burning down of a cabin, also at the mouth of Napoleon along the river, where his half-brother was sleeping. No wonder the troopers called us the Napoleon Creek gang.

They had mistaken us for the ones who were responsible for the summons. We went along with the assumption!

Before the trooper visit, Mom and I had planned a big party for Thursday, which was my birthday. We decided to have the party on Monday. That way, Brenda and her husband, Charles, could be there. They would leave on Tuesday to have time on Wednesday in Fairbanks to get a lawyer for court Thursday morning at 8 a.m.

Kurt took an empty barrel upriver. The party began without him. By the time he returned, all nine of us were wasted. When we noticed that he had two guys in the boat with two rifles, handguns hanging all over them, and enough ammo to shoot the top off any mountain, we became a little bit apprehensive.

The guys were messengers, sent to tell us that seven members of the Russell family were coming down, half by water, half by land, to take over the camp and shoot down any resistors. Talk about excitement! An edge was put on our partying, which we continued, since we were already three sheets to the wind.

We discussed all sorts of survival tactics, such as "go for cover, not concealment." I decided to stick with the Vietnam vets, thinking they would be the ones to live through this if anyone did. About 2 a.m., I said goodnight to the one guy who was going to stay up all night.

The Russells did not show up that night. They had indeed started out but had run into some rocks with their too-big-for-this-river, 24-foot, canopied, 115HP-propelled boat. Their trip was cut short when they got hung up on the same big rock that Carole and I had been hung up on three years before, a mile down from the bridge. After barely making it out of the launch area, their trip came to an end. Whew! Excitement and no gun play made this one of the best, if not the best, birthday parties I ever had. Also, I was not certain why they wanted to come down and shoot us up when we were all going to be in court in three days where the issue would be settled peacefully.

We all went to court on Thursday. The plaintiff, whose name on the summons no one recognized, turned out to be the Russells' new stepdad, DeWayne. All the Russells were in disguise, with dyed hair and aliases. We knew who they were, though they were hiding behind the new name. The court decision went against them. Consequently, no one had to move camp or do any other thing.

However, Charles hurried back to the river to move his camp across the river despite the court decision. He did not want to be near the Russells. As it was, the Russell-Princes were allowed by the court to dredge on the same claim as the dredgers they had attempted to displace.

Kurt and I went on to Anchorage where Mom caught a plane home. She was reluctant to leave, as she had never had a vacation like this one.

By the time Kurt and I returned a week later, we had new neighbors about 50 feet away where Charles and Brenda had been.

The new neighbors, Bob and DeWayne and their various and sundry divers, did not speak to us at first. Since moving was such a pain, and we weren't dredging on the claim they said they had leased from the Russells, we decided to stay.

I tried to approach the macho DeWayne, but he was cold and uncommunicative. I broke down and cried from sheer frustration in front of all their camp, and the ice was broken! I guess some men like women to be crybabies because Bob and the other divers afterward became friendly. As the weeks went by, even DeWayne was friendly enough to confide that Bob was okay when sober but watch out when he was drinking.

The friendliest of all was DeWayne's wife, who would not tell me her name. She asked me to call her Mom, though I was much older than she. I was in the uncomfortable position of not calling her by any name, just saying "Hey" when I wanted her attention. I was not supposed to know her name, so I did not push the issue.

I noticed, though, that Bob's hair was changing colors after he had been diving for a couple of weeks. Hmm. DeWayne's blond wife, "Mom," who came down after the guys settled in, soon showed some very dark roots. Hmm. One of Bob's friends from Fairbanks came to visit, and two times in Kurt's and my tent, called Bob, Dave. Hmm.

I asked Kurt if he had noticed. He had. We talked about what we were going to do with the information. Before we could decide, Bob-Dave came over for coffee and said his name was Robert David. Me thinks the man protests too much! As it turned out, "Bob" was David Russell and "Mom" was Judy Russell-Prince, and Kurt and I were in the lion's den.

Later that day, Rod Knight boated up, stopped where "Mom," and I were talking on the beach, and said, "I know who you are, Judy Russell," thus opening that can of worms, once and for all.

David had been acquitted of shooting the two unarmed men in the back, nine and eleven times, respectively, around Christmas 1978. His defense was self-defense. One juror made the statement that he had such an innocent face he must be innocent! David's partner was convicted and went to prison.

In March of 1981, the cabin David and his half-brother were staying in burned to the ground. Coleman lantern fuel was the reputed cause of the fire. David was fully clothed, standing outside at 4 a.m., while Leonard, the brother, was asleep and got burned over 90 percent of his body. He lived but was hospitalized a long time. David's cot was at the back of the cabin. In order to get out, he had to pass his brother's cot.

This family hired a lawyer to take care of the claim. During the winter, the lawyer forgot to file the necessary paperwork for claim maintenance, and the claim reverted to the BLM. The Russell-Princes were not seen on the river again.

The summer of 1982 was juicy enough for a lifetime. I am pretty sure that anyone who was there that summer never forgot it!

Judy had extended an offer to me to provide a bulldozer-dug hole in the bench the next summer to put my dredge in. She did this, she said, because I was a woman. She knew what it meant to be out there in that man's world. I was touched by her understanding. I was sorry they lost the claim. Who knows how that would have worked out. The temptation to work in that nugget area in virgin ground was food for dreams! Thank you, Judy, for your kindness.

That summer was a low water year. For 30 days, there were no boats going up or down the river. Usually, when boats ran the river, we heard the motor for 10 minutes before we caught sight of the boat. The huge quiet carried sounds long distances. During the month of quiet, we all heard ghost boats, boats which never arrived. When the water came up, Rod Knight came upriver in the first boat. We had no doubt his was a real boat. That was the end of the ghost boats for that summer. Little things were notable in our world of few civilization noises.

Gold mining is definitely not typical girl work. I had much money/time invested in it. While hanging in there when things weren't right, I loved it when things were running well. Most of the time, we were by ourselves in camp, so my being a woman was usually accepted, though I ran into condescension and harassment from one of the members of our team. Over the years, I also experienced sexual harassment and coercion from several miners.

Most miners we socialized with seemed glad to have a female point of view. That said, once that summer, a member of a nearby camp took exception to my presence for reasons unknown and poured a quart of oil in our dredge hole. This could have created a major problem if we had not noticed and had started the engines. Oil would have got into the sluice box, causing the gold we dredged up to slide on through the box, as well as being a royal pain to clean out. I suppose if the guy had meant serious business, he would have poured the oil directly into the sluice box. Or maybe, he was too dumb or a coward, messing around with people he considered unlikely to respond, which we didn't.

At the end of the season, Rich and crew stopped by our camp while on their last trip of the season. All summer I had asked myself if Rich was the best dredger on the river, and did he have a drinking problem. The answers were yes and no. I decided to check him out. During this visit, we each noticed the other. I had known Rich three summers by the time electricity sparked between us. He went to Australia that winter; I went to Eagle River, Alaska, near Anchorage. The fire between us smoldered all winter.

*L to R: Rich Goodson, Clyde Miles, Gary Goodson, and Carter Jahn
who worked for Kurt and me a short time in 1982.*

12. Butte Creek 1983

During a visit to Memphis in late April, I met a college senior who was graduating in a couple of weeks. He thought he would like to take the summer and try gold mining in Alaska before tackling his career in the fall. I tried to test his commitment to this idea by playing devil's advocate with a few reality checks, mainly how remote this situation was. He would not be dissuaded.

So, on May 17, Michael Pasquale and his brother, Scott, flew into Anchorage, Alaska. Kurt and I picked them up at the airport and headed north.

That night, we got to Eagle Trail Campground, nine miles south of Tok, pulled in and made our beds. One person slept in the truck, one bedded on top of the picnic table under a blue tarp, one was on the ground under the table, and I don't remember where the other one slept. I do remember waking up with two inches of snow on the blue tarp. The falling snow had not awakened me. Welcome to Alaska, boys!

We went on, through Chicken at MP 67 on the Taylor Highway, to the lower landing at South Fork bridge at MP 75, then downriver to our camp from last year at Napoleon. In the next three days, we arranged for Scott to work with Donnie Snyder and Roy George above Napoleon.

Kurt, Mike, and I gathered up our stashed camping gear and dredge equipment and headed for our new camp down below Butte. By this time Rich Goodson owned the claim. By an agreement with him, we would work his ground and give him a percentage of whatever we recovered.

Kurt was driving the square-stern canoe fitted with a boat motor. We had packed the canoe as full as possible. Michael and I were rafting the overloaded dredge containing the rest of our gear. As we figured out how to keep from crashing the dredge into cliffs, we grew overconfident.

We had gone six miles when we were swept to the left side of the river above Buckskin Creek. As a result we got high centered on a big flat rock up against the cliff, with the front of the dredge tilted into the river. Within moments, our gear stacked on the dredge began washing off into the river. There was nothing we could do. The slightest movement caused more items to slide overboard.

Meanwhile, Kurt had taken the canoe load ahead to our campsite, six miles further downriver. By the time he unloaded and returned, we had been standing for an hour on the back of the dredge, straining to keep the front balanced above the water level to keep as few of our possessions as possible from floating away. Kurt captured most of the floataways.

In an attempt to lighten the load enough to get off high center and floating again, we loaded the canoe from the pile on the dredge. By this time, it was too late to make another canoe trip down to Butte. We slept on the shelf-shaped rock ledges at the bottom of the cliff. They were narrow, hard, and cold.

The next day we did not float the dredge again until the canoe had made several back-and-forth trips. We now managed to float the empty dredge the rest of the way with much more maneuverability and control. We got partly stuck once. I jumped off and gave it a shove before it could get solidly stuck. We were too close to our camp for any more delays.

On June 15, Mike left after almost three weeks. As our boat was not operational (again), Mike decided to take his large backpack and hike to Napoleon 14 miles upriver. We urged him to wait until we could figure some way to take him up, but he left.

We were 14 isolated miles down from the activity at Napoleon, where his brother was. He could not get to the post office often enough to keep up with his girlfriend in Tennessee. So, after we had driven 800 miles round trip to Anchorage to pick him up, he was gone, and we were going to be without another diver on the dredge. Again. It is hard to find people who stick with it.

Later, we heard that he had barely made it around the corner from our camp before a crisis occurred. While trying to walk across a steep rockslide area, he and his pack slid off into a deep water eddy. The pack kept weighing him down to the bottom. He would kick himself back up to the surface. He managed to get the straps loose and discard the pack, allowing him control of the situation. In the process, he lost his glasses.

Being determined to get to Napoleon, he did not come back to our camp, so we were unaware of his trials. As I have said before, sometimes things work out in unexpected ways. As he set off, a boat with a few guys on a joyride came by. The driver of the boat, Roy George from Napoleon, was just about ready to turn around and go back up when he saw Mike! What a sight that must have been. A wet hiker in the middle of nowhere does not compute. As far as they knew, he had nowhere to be coming from. The next bridge was 20 miles away.

Mike worked at Napoleon with his brother until they got enough gold to go home to Memphis. Roy and his crew took the brothers to Fairbanks to catch their plane. We wondered whether they knew how much they had cost all of us in time and money by having to go get them, then take them places when we had dredging to do. The driving alone for both trips was 1,400 miles! The time spent doing so was costly also.

Butte was too far downriver for Mike's needs. He had helped us get the dredge downriver, part of getting set up for dredging. We were grateful for that.

I have included this to show how important every day is in the short Alaskan dredging season. By the time Mike left Kurt and me, a month had passed, and we were almost back where we started in mid-May, without a diver and with no prospects for getting another one.

July 11, 1983: Kurt went up to Rich's camp to see if anyone would come down and work with us.

July 29: Rich came and spent the night.

August 7: Rich moved down to Kurt's and my camp. So began a 15-year association. From then on our mining crew was some combination of Rich's brother Gary, Clyde Miles, Joe Taylor, my brother Kurt, Rich, and me.

Once or twice over the years, we had one camp, and other times we had two camps far apart on different forks of the 40 Mile.

August 8: Kurt and Rich began dredging together, using my 8" dredge, mining gear, boat, and camp.

September 5: Hail

September 7: Snow

September 15: Auroras, cold night: 20°F

September 17: Cracked head gasket on dredge engine

September 22: Rain, rain, rain

September 23: More snow, float out. Night at 40 Mile bridge.

September 24: Night near South Fork bridge at Rainbow Camp, a Cat mining camp set up that one summer by wealthy apple growers from Wenatchee, WA, who had decided to try their hand at gold mining.

They had a landing strip, hot running water, microwave, VCR, heaters in the tents, and many other amenities. When we saw these comforts of civilization, we thought we were hallucinating. None of us had ever considered that these luxuries were possible on the river.

They even had a cook who went to town 90 miles away once or twice a week. Then he came back and cooked for their workers. There were fresh greens, a sight that made us feel like country cousins. Thanks to them for taking us in for those two days, feeding us and giving us tents with heaters!

13. SNOW IN AUGUST 1984

Rich, Clyde, and I worked at Butte Creek area. The summer was pretty drama free. After Rich and Clyde went to Anchorage for four days, August 14-17, we began dredging again. That lasted two days, until Clyde built a fire in the wood stove in the tent where we put wet diving gear to dry or at least get warm. Because the fire was slow taking off, Clyde opened the stove door to speed things up, then left and came up to the kitchen where Rich and I were.

In a few minutes, we noticed black smoke coming from the area of the warm-up tent. When we ran down, the whole tent had burned and with it, the wetsuits, booties, gloves, and everything else except the stove. Since by then it was August 19, and the season was coming to an end, we discussed whether to replace the gear or quit for the season. Ultimately, we decided to continue since we were in good gold.

Now it was my turn to go to Anchorage for the replacement of what had burned since they had just come back from there. They would borrow gear to limp through until I came back.

On the 20th Rich took me upriver and dropped me off. I headed for Anchorage where I rounded up the new suits and other gear. I left my truck in Anchorage with Ross so it would be there for wintertime use and took the bus back to Tok on Saturday August 25.

The bus driver and the people on the bus would spend the night in the local motel. The driver told me he would drop me off the next day at Tetlin Junction where the Taylor Highway begins if I would wait until then. So I spent the night in the motel too since I did not want to hitchhike at that late hour.

On Sunday, snow was falling in Tok but had not covered the ground. In spite of the snow, I was going to hitchhike from the junction to Chicken or South Fork. As I stood there waiting for some vehicle to come and turn onto the Taylor, snowfall kept increasing. I was not worried. In the summertime, many tourists and locals use the road.

The first vehicle to come by picked me up. It was a motorhome with four men and a woman, non-English-speaking Germans, with two 60-pound Airedale dogs. I added my cargo to their rig and got in. We set about getting to know each other as much as was possible under the circumstances.

The first 10 miles of the Taylor Highway are uphill. With the wet, heavy snowfall getting more intense, we began to notice cracking noises made by the breaking and falling trees around us. We went forward with shivers of fear as we realized a tree could fall on the RV.

At MP 8, we got stuck in the deepening snow. We tried to back up. Nothing. There was no going forward, either. We got out to assess the situation at the exact moment a tree fell across the road behind us.

My hosts were a merry group and took this in stride. Their solution was to make soup and have a meal, all possible without much inconvenience because we were in a motorhome. While we were eating, we heard a vehicle coming up behind us. We got out to see the Alaska DOT crew with a grader and a dump truck behind it to pull the grader out if it got stuck.

The grader pushed the tree off the road and went around us, clearing the road. We could now get going again with minimal shoveling. The DOT crew told us we were the last vehicle on the road before they had closed it down at the junction. They also said the Germans would have to turn around, but I could go on with DOT in the dump truck.

I said my thanks, got my gear transferred and climbed in. As we drove on, we rescued 15 vehicles stuck along the road. The drivers of those vehicles had to turn around and go back to Tok or if they were pointed in the direction of Tok, they proceeded there. Once we got to MP 34, the high point on that part of the Taylor, the snow disappeared.

They took me on to MP 56, where John Burns, who worked for DOT on the Chicken section of the road, lived with his family. His wife, Kathy, fed me. A sense of normalcy surrounded me after an unusual morning.

After hanging out with this friendly family and catching up on local news, John took me to the South Fork bridge at MP 75 where Rich was waiting.

There was no more snow on the road, but snow had also fallen on the river. Most of the tents went down in the night due to the heavy snow.

Rich told me our tent had fallen an inch from his face at 1 a.m., which at that time of year is in darkness. He said to himself that he would deal with it in the morning and went back to sleep.

August 25, 1984. Wet Snow at Butte Creek Camp. Many tents along the river collapsed that night.

We worked until September 28. Then, we spent three days cleaning gold and putting the dredge and camp away. The next three days were spent getting up to the landing and leaving for Fairbanks. By this time the calendar had changed to October. We were barely ahead of the winter weather. A week later, the temperature was 0°F, and a week after that, the temperature was -11°F. By the end of October weather in the Interior of Alaska means business.

Janice and Rich, summer of 1984

14. DAILY ROUTINE

A typical dredger's camp: Sleeping tent on left. Hootch on right. Very few had vehicles though. Most did not have road access to their camp.

Some years, when Rich and I worked with others, I was the cook and camp tender. Other years when it was just we two, the routine was slightly different.

In the big camps, everyone was responsible for his own breakfast and lunch. If there were leftovers from dinner the night before, they incorporated them into their lunch. Otherwise, they started from scratch. After buzzing around at breakfast time for an hour or so, they left for the day of dredging.

When they were gone, I began my day. I did the final clean-up of the gold from the day before, a chore that took several hours. I gathered and bucked up wood for the wood stove. I thought pretty much all day about what I was going to cook for dinner. I strove at all times to keep the menu varied and interesting. As some of you know, that takes a lot of thinking. Plus, there were no pizza delivery places or nearby restaurants to take the load off.

Each summer the various members of our team had particular items they were not eating. One diver did not want wheat. One diver was a vegetarian. Another was not eating dairy. I did not mind the challenge of cooking around these requests. I would cook something like brown rice and beans and vegetables in one pan, and canned salmon entree in another pan. Everyone took whatever he was currently eating.

We took with us enough food for the whole summer. Mostly, I used Rich's and my food when cooking for everybody, though the guys brought food too, which they mainly used for breakfast and lunch if they did not want leftovers or if there weren't any.

I could keep many vegetables and fruits in a cardboard box, stuck under a spruce tree where rain would not get on it. I sometimes spread a plastic cover over the box, just in case, when we had a multi-day downpour. Never once did any animal get into the veggie box. There were potatoes, onions, carrots, winter squashes, apples, oranges, lemons, garlic, and a few other foods that have a long shelf life, which when stored properly would last all summer in the box.

Trips to Tok or Fairbanks supplemented the lettuce, bananas, and other less hardy fruits and vegetables. We had enough in camp to make it through the summer without frills. Lots of veggies and meats come in cans, so we had plenty of canned items. Did you know whole chickens come in cans? And bacon? I did not, at first. I will say those chickens don't taste that great once the novelty has worn off, and the bacon is unimaginably salty until it is washed.

Alaska supplied blueberries, cranberries, and raspberries, in season.

Alaska also supplied a cooler for storing cheese, butter, bacon, and eggs. Here's how: Certain land areas in Alaska are frozen starting about four inches below the surface in a layer called permafrost which can be quite deep. We would remove the sod in the shape of the hole we wanted, exposing the frozen ground. We let it thaw for a day or two, then removed the soupy thawed layer, exposing and thawing the next layer of ice, over and over until we had a hole deep enough to accommodate a 5-gallon bucket with a lid, loaded with our cooler items. We used various techniques to cover the hole to seal in the cold temperature. Sometimes, we covered the bucket with plastic to keep the lid cleaner and a plywood cover to keep dirt and animals out, though bears have been known to get in anyway.

Our cold hole, as this nifty "appliance" is called, was not broken into by bears. However, I remember one camp's crew had just come back from restocking in town 100 miles away and had three or four slabs of bacon stolen from their cold hole by a bear or bears unknown. Thinking about it now still hurts, 40 years later. Lots of us love bacon, don't we? So, why wouldn't a bear!

In the middle of the afternoon, I began cooking so dinner would be ready whenever the guys got home. I would start cleaning that day's gold when they came in so I could get as much as possible done by bedtime. After a day of not seeing them, I still would miss out on the conversation because the gold cleaning area was in another part of camp than the living room tent and kitchen.

Those were the summers where I did not make any money on the dredge and by default, became the camp cook. Only once did any one of them give me any gold for my camp tender trouble. I guess the others felt that I was Rich's tag-along, so he would take care of me. I took care of them anyway. I was all in on the mining career, whether I was working on the dredge or in the camp.

The years that it was just Rich and me, we did a lot of things together. I enjoyed those mining seasons especially. Rich was a great cook. He would share the cooking, which was mental as well as physical relief since I did not have to think so much about cooking.

Plus, I got a percentage when participating in the actual dredging, as opposed to working in camp. I loved the one-on-one. Our dredge days were on our clock. We worked during the best part of the day, spending three, four or five hours at the dredge. Since he did not have to work around other divers, Rich's dredging days were much shorter than theirs were. They were still long, full days.

When three guys were working on one dredge, one would be diving for three hours, one would be tending for three hours, and one would be having down time for three hours. Then, they would change around until all three had done each job for three hours, a total of nine hours. The emptying of the first four feet of the sluice for cleanup took another hour. Barring any mechanical downtime, this took a minimum of 10 hours.

When Rich and I were working together, I pumped the gas for the day from a 55-gallon barrel into 5-gallon containers, packed the food for the day, battened down the camp by putting away all food for varmint deterrence, zipped up the tents in case of rain, gathered clothing for any weather because we would not be back until we were done dredging, and carried out many other seemingly small preparations to make it all work. Rich serviced the boat motor and got gas for the boat tank and made sure he had all of his diving gear.

On the dredge, while Rich was underwater, I finished cleaning the gold, and if necessary, repaired wetsuits, moved tailing piles, kept rocks from piling up in the sluice box, helped to remove rocks stuck in the dredge hose, kept tabs on the gas and time, and on really good days when everything worked smoothly, I did exercises or read a book.

I battled mosquitoes, rain, snow, gnats, wind, and exhaust from the two engines. When the diver came up and needed something, I tried to understand the him as he talked through a face mask as engines roared and rocks bounced off of the metal parts inside the dredge, as well as the sounds of the river. A whole system of gestures, grunts, hand waving and slapping the water developed over years. This "language" could be added to under new circumstances. That's when the fun began. It was like charades.

Being on the dredge was mostly solitary work since the diver could be out of verbal communication for hours at a time. This lent a meditative quality to the work. I would watch the river flow, something it did with a great deal of peace generated by the quiet beauty of the scene. The silence competed with the noise of the dredge against which I wore hearing protection.

All things were securely tied to the dredge. Before I learned that, I had seen my favorite hat blow away, had turned around to see my lawn chair floating off down the river, or had found only one dive glove when there should have been two on the dredge platform.

Sometimes, when we went downriver looking for an item blown off by wind or blasting water from the hose or vibration of the dredge, we would find it in an eddy or a bush somewhere. Other things were never seen again. Our river runs into the Yukon, and 1,000 miles down the Yukon is the Bering Sea. The good news was that heavier things like tools generally fell in and stayed close to the dredge on the bottom of the river. Not much got away. We needed all of it.

A Roger Tallini Observation:

A dredger's hands are always cut up and/or dry and cracked from being wet and dried and calloused. By season's end, one's hands are in pretty rough shape. Also, the tools you have left by the end of the season are a far cry less than what you had at the beginning. We would always lose screwdrivers, wrenches and ratchets in the river and in the tundra. Both the tundra and water just swallowed up tools.

Donnie Snyder and I had a saying that when you arrived at the 40 Mile at the beginning of the season, you needed to grab a screwdriver, lay your hands on the rocks and jab your hands and fingers repeatedly until they bled. Then take your box of tools down to the river and throw them into the water. We figured we might as well get the pain and the loss of tools over with to set the mood for dredging. Ha!

Roger told me they would go back to camp at the end of the day and apply mercurochrome to their wounded hands, screaming as they dabbed because that is the way mercurochrome works.

I have to say that I never thought of applying a screwdriver to my cut up, cracked hands or using mercurochrome. We used hydrogen peroxide for lots of things or let nature's healing powers do its thing. But there can be more than one solution to lots of problems...

15. MISADVENTURES

This first story concerns Wes and Randy DeVore. They were making runs down from the South Fork landing, testing out their new boat and motor on a rainy day with thunder rumbling and lightning flashing.

L to R: Wes and Randy DeVore

The first run was uneventful. Randy and the gear were left at what would be Donnie Snyder's camp, six miles down. Several times during the trip, rain intensified for a few minutes.

The second load was heavy, 700 to 800 pounds, containing a microwave, small refrigerator, industrial-size tent, and other camp gear, as well as a gas tank for Donnie's Mercury boat motor. Wes could see over the huge load piled three feet high in the middle of the boat, which is always a good thing.

As he approached a set of rapids, he noticed the gas in his boat tank was low. Because of this heavy load, he decided to change over to Donnie's boat gas tank before trying to negotiate the treacherous rapids ahead. In the quiet water above the rapids, he found that his Evinrude tank hookup would not connect to Donnie's Mercury setup. Therefore, he started pouring the Merc gas into his Evinrude tank without a funnel, spilling gas inside the boat.

When the tank was half full, with the boat rocking as he moved around, the tanks touched, creating a static electric charge, which caused both gas tanks to burst into flames, sending up a cloud of black smoke.

Wes threw his tank overboard. Because it was still connected to the engine by the gas hose, the tank stayed close to the boat. A three-foot ring of fire surged around the boat as the gas spread quickly over the water.

The gas tank in the boat was also on fire. Wes threw it out of the boat. The gas in the bottom of the boat was on fire, too. Boat gas is mixed with oil which slows the burning, allowing the fire to burn longer.

Wes had lined up the boat toward the navigable part of the rapids before trying to change the gas tanks. This made his trip through the rapids somewhat less dangerous. Without an engine to steer the boat, he would have bounced off of more rocks than he did if he had not aimed it. At one point, he remembers hitting a rock with the side of the boat which increased his chances of swamping the boat, especially with his load. Going through rapids sideways is always dangerous.

After he contemplated jumping overboard, he clambered up to the front of the boat to grab the paddle and maybe guide all of this to the riverbank. The change of balance in the boat brought the fire forward, as the gas and water shifted to the front.

At that moment, the sky opened up. The cloudburst lasted 30 intense seconds, during which he had to put his hand up over his nose to create a place to breathe in the wall of water coming out of the sky. The rain overfilled the boat with water, washing the remaining gas fire overboard, thus extinguishing the fire in the boat.

But now, the boat was full of water. He grabbed the rope tied to the front of the boat and threw it into an overhanging tree. The rope caught, bringing the boat close enough for him to jump to shore. He happened to be on the left side of the river going down, which was the side Donnie's camp was on, one mile further. He decided to walk to the camp, not really having any alternative because the boat was now full of water and without gas to move it down. Under the water in the boat, the boat was covered in a black, oily, sooty film, as was everything in it.

When he got down to Randy, who was under a tarp trying to stay dry, Wes said, "I have some good news and some bad news. The good news is I am still alive."

Randy said, "OMG, let me guess. The bad news is you are burned."

Wes: "No, I am not burned."

Randy: "Your face and clothing are covered with something black."

The fire had singed off Wes' eyebrows, eyelashes, and hair back one inch from his face. His face and clothing were covered with black soot from the initial burst of fire. He and Randy hiked back to the boat, bailed it out, and floated it down to the camp. At least, that is what Wes thinks happened. He was in shock and doesn't really remember how the boat got to camp. Part of the bad news was the microwave had melted.

Another Wes and Randy Adventure

Later that same summer, we were awakened at 1 a.m. by the sound in the distance of a boat motor. When the boat arrived in the dark, Wes and Randy tumbled out, wet and soggy. Their story is typical of the types of things that happened to all of us but particularly to them!

They had set out from their camp at 10 p.m. to test their negw boat motor after earlier burning up the last one, driving the new one seven miles downriver past us, the last camp on this part of the river. Going so far put them further out of the way of help should they need any. 10 p.m. is pretty late to go so far afield. Plus, the water was high, which in the daylight might be a good thing, but in the darkening light, bad things can happen.

Wanting to see what was on this part of the river, they had boated down past us and on through the confluence, then turned around at Long Bar, two or three more miles down. As they came back through the confluence, which was turbulent at this water depth and full of rollers, Wes revved up the engine to full throttle and made it over the first roller. At great speed, the boat nosed down in between the first and second rollers, pushing up a big wave, which they roared into. The wave filled the boat with water, swamping but not sinking it.

They were able to keep going forward very slowly in the rolling water. Before anything else happened, Wes decided to pull over to bail the water out of the boat. He made too steep a turn, causing the water inside the boat to rush to one side. The uneven load dipped that side of the boat under the water. The boat turned over in the middle of the flooding confluence. Wes was thrown out. Randy, momentarily pinned under the boat, was able to grab a life vest. Randy was able to get out from under the boat and hold on to one side of the boat. So, while Wes held on to the other side, they floated down the river. During these big floods, the river water goes toward the middle of the river with such strength that they were unable to maneuver to shore.

That very day they had tied a 50-foot rope to the bow of the boat. As they floated, Wes was able to get the end of the rope, and as they went around a big bend in the river, the current carried them toward the shore. There, Wes was able stand up, plant his feet, and swing the boat to shore. During all this time, they became super cold, causing their reflexes to slow.

At 11 p.m., visibility, even in the long Alaskan summer light, was limited. However, they were able to get the boat toward the beach far enough to turn it over. Unfortunately, this scooped up water, filling the boat three fourths full.

Before going any further, they had to turn their attention to making a fire. Randy said he did not even notice anymore how cold he was; he just felt overwhelmingly tired, a characteristic of hypothermia. They were also being attacked by millions of mosquitoes, which smoke might deter. They made a circle of gas from the boat tank, still attached by the rubber hose connecting the tank to the boat motor.

As happened to them many times, the one thing they needed, they had. Randy had a lighter in his pocket. With cold hands and wet lighter, he tried and tried to light the lighter before the gas on the sand evaporated. Finally, a spark lit the fire and soon, they were warm enough to think about the boat situation.

They located a tomato paste can on the riverbank, converting it from river trash to bailer. That is four ounces of water being emptied out of the boat at a time, little better than nothing and astonishingly time consuming. As one bailed, the other warmed himself in the fire circle.

After an hour, when the boat was half empty, they turned their attention to getting the motor started again. They had attached a toolbox to the seat of the boat but had not latched it when they started on this adventure. Consequently, their tools fell out into the river when the boat turned over. As they examined the situation, they found the ratchet and attached spark plug socket caught in the steering cables of the boat. They had angels watching over them, because without being able to take the spark plug out and dry it, they would not have been able to start the engine. Then they would have had to hike the four or five miles up to our camp in the dark for help.

They pushed the boat back into the flooding river and started the engine. When they were going fast enough, they pulled the two drain plugs out of the back of the boat for self-bailing, which occurs when a boat goes fast enough to let the water run out. If one pulls the plug with the boat standing still, the boat sinks. It takes a while for half a boatload of water to self-bail.

After they arrived at our camp, they sat by the wood stove, telling us about what had happened to them since we last saw them going down the river. Finally warm enough, and not wanting to spend the night, they borrowed some dry socks and took off in the dark.

Though we were not boaters who usually traveled in the dark, sometimes it occurred due to happenstance. One rule to follow might be: When you have a choice, do not start out at 10 p.m. on a flooding river on a joyride.

Joe Taylor's Tale

Joe Taylor used to tell this story in camp. In 1981, one of Joe's partners, Tom Davis of Fallon, NV and Joe took Tom's truck to Fairbanks to get supplies and do laundry. Joe's clean clothes were in a plastic bag in the truck bed, as were the groceries. They also brought back six cans of Blazo (white gas for cookstoves), several full boat gas tanks, and a battery with side posts.

As they were bouncing up the washboard Taylor Highway along Jack Wade Creek after stopping at South Fork to pick up the boat and motor, and putting the boat upside down on the truck rack and the motor inside the bed, Joe dozed off.

Suddenly, the calm was broken by Tom slamming on the brakes and yelling "Fire!"

As Joe was waking up, trying to decide whether to get away from the truck or try to put the fire out, Tom jumped into the back of truck and began throwing burning things onto the road. After throwing a few things out, he left that flaming pile and drove the truck ahead, hoping to avoid a bigger explosion. Then, he went back to the bed of the truck to throw more burning items onto the road. In total, there were three piles of flaming items as he had pulled ahead three times. The first pile contained the Blazo; it blew up from the intense heat, sending a mushroom cloud of black smoke into the air. The other two fires which contained the gas tanks also exploded.

A Cat miner saw the three smoke clouds and came over on his bulldozer with three fire extinguishers. Neither the first nor the second extinguisher worked! The third one worked. Joe had been tasked with getting the fire extinguishers into action. The Cat miner scooped up wet gravel and dumped it on the three smoldering piles, putting out the rest of the fires. It looked like a war zone.

The boat motor mount, made of wood, was incinerated. The cowling and wiring of the motor melted. The food and laundry they got in town burned up. And Tom's hands were burned.

They found the battery had slid forward with all the bouncing around, smashed into a boat gas tank, punching two post holes in the side of the tank. This sparked off a fire, at the same time releasing the gas, already on fire, to run out into the truck bed.

The truck had a full 40-gallon reserve tank, which hissed while the fire was intense but miraculously did not explode. The back of the truck and inside of the boat was charred as was everything else.

They went back to the landing at South Fork, where Tom dropped off Joe. Because the fire was the last straw for Tom, he decided then and there to pull up stakes and go home to Nevada while he still had a truck. First, he went back to Fairbanks to the doctor!

Phil Schmidt helped Joe. After Joe cleaned his boat, he went to Tok and got parts to repair the motor.

After a few days, when he got down to the cabin at the confluence, he was wearing his only clothes. He did not have any others; his clean laundry had burned up in the fire.

While he was telling the story to his brother, Glenn, and their father, Smoky, he saw a plastic bag washed up on the beach below the cabin, of all the places it could have floated to along the 35 miles of river between the bridges. When he opened the bag, he found clothes: long johns, a pair of pants exactly like the ones he lost in the fire except four inches longer, and tee shirts.

At first, he wondered how his clothes had floated home. Then, he realized they were not his, but they fit. He put the pants on and rolled up the legs. No one on the river or in Chicken walked up to him and identified them as the summer went on. The universe had provided for his needs.

In 1979, Joe found an unopened package of Oscar Meyer wieners washed up on the same beach, which he cooked and ate!

Joe, Glenn, and Smoky Taylor dredged up six ounces of gold in 30 hours, their first. They still have that gold on display in their store in Fairbanks.

Roger Tallini's Dredge Moving Story Told by Roger

The perils of dredging alone go unsaid. Simply moving your dredge can be a monumental undertaking. I was at my Gibraltar Rock claim, right above rough water and Deadman's Curve, a place where the river took a sharp turn, and the current could smash you into the canyon wall.

I needed to move my dredge to the other side of the river, but I was working alone and floating the dredge to the other side before the current took me into Deadman's Curve would be impossible.

I came up with the idea of tying a rope to a tree on the other side of the river, attaching it to the dredge and letting the dredge float across. I took the canoe over to the other side of the river, tied a rope to a tree, put the rope in the canoe and paddled back to the dredge. I tied the rope to the dredge taking up as much slack in the rope as I could. I prepared for the worst because the water was high and fast.

I fired up the dredge and began propelling myself to the other side. As I progressed, much better than I imagined, the rope slackened and went under the dredge. The current was swift on the other side when I got there. The dredge quickly began floating downriver. The slack in the rope tightened under the dredge, rapidly throwing it up on one side of the pontoons. I was thrown across the jet tubes as the dredge tilted to a 45 degree angle, about ready to flip. I grabbed a box cutter I had attached with a lanyard to the frame of the dredge and cut the rope.

When I cut the rope, the dredge plunged back down in the water. Since I was already over at the bank but freely floating downriver, I jumped up and dropped the stiff leg. The stiff leg dragged along the bottom for 10 feet or so until it held fast. I got off, tied up the dredge with another rope that was attached to the dredge. I assessed the damage. The right front pontoon was indented from the rope...that was it.

After it was over, I realized how blessed I was to have that box cutter within arm's reach because if the dredge had flipped, it would have been on top of me.

Rich Goodson Tangles with the Falls

Forty six years into it and having seen almost everything, Rich was not immune to the extremes of river living. Recently, after breakup while the river was still high and cold, he and Clyde were boating up through the falls, a class III rapids, when the water caught the front end of the boat and folded it back on itself. At the ripe old age of 77, he found himself dumped into the 36°F water in the heart of the most infamous rapids on the American part of the Mainstem, along with Clyde. People have died in these rapids. Every trip up or down the falls fills boaters with anxiety.

They were wearing life jackets and made it to shore. Clyde lost his boots. He improvised footwear by duct taping his feet into neoprene gloves in an effort to warm his cold feet. Pretty clever solution.

The dredgers who happened along shortly thereafter helped to straighten out the boat. They used ratchet straps to hold the gunnels (sides) in line, allowing Rich and Clyde immediate use of the boat.

A week later before a run up through the falls, Rich decided to assess the situation. He pulled the boat into the eddy at the bottom of the rapids. When he had determined where the channel was, he pulled into the current at too wide an angle. The boat was immediately swamped.

Everything in the loaded boat, including loose items and some totes containing gear floated away, while heavier stuff sank to the river bottom.

Miners hanging around the launch area a mile downstream which Rich had just left, saw the contents of the boat floating by and jumped into action. They rescued most of the gear. Then, they went upstream to see what had happened.

Rich and Clyde somehow managed to get to the side of the river, but the boat was sunk.

When I last heard, the boat with motor was a twisted, sunken piece of river junk which the river had pushed into the eddy at the end of the rapids.

Rich is an experienced boat driver who has driven through the falls many times over the years. The river did not care. In one moment, the river spoke its eternal truth: I'm the boss. Pay attention. Experience only goes so far.

At least, he did this in a grand manner!

Even at relatively low water, the rapids look challenging enough.

These seven rocks are the backbone of the terrible rapids.
It's mind-blowing to see them at this record low water.

16. Karma and Claim Jumping

I am not certain of the year, but around 1987, Kurt, Rich and I camped at Voss Creek, where they were dredging around the corner at the end of the Napoleon Creek straightaway. The claim they were working was the last in the straightaway, an area with lots of nuggets. This was an unusual occurrence since gold was usually fines or dust. We were all excited every day because of the nuggets, a gold miner's dream come true.

One day, they came back to camp for lunch, saying they were at the end of our claim and faced a moral dilemma because they needed to quit at the claim line. The claim above belonged to Donnie Snyder or Nicky Bass. Nicky had given them permission to dredge on the claim, but the ownership of the claim was in a gray area. I joined in their discussion, encouraging them to go over the line just a little distance to finish the day and get their hours in. They could then go up to Nicky's camp and figure out the specifics. Wouldn't everybody do that? When they went back after lunch, they decided to go ahead and dredge on Donnie's claim since Nicky had given them permission through some confusion about who owned the claim.

In the way of the universe, Wes and Randy were coming downriver at exactly that time and heard the dredge running. They dropped a load off a mile up from where Kurt and Rich were dredging and went back upriver. During a conversation with Donnie when they ran into him and Roger Tallini, they mentioned that they had heard a dredge running in the general vicinity of Napoleon straightaway.

Donnie and Roger decided to go down and check it out. They caught Rich and Kurt red-handed.

Donnie said the immortal words, "Drop your box!" In dredging lingo, this means empty the sluice box back into the river. Our box had many hours on it from the legal mining on our own claim. Rich and Kurt managed to talk Donnie into agreeing to go right then up to Nicky's camp. Nicky confirmed that he had given Rich permission. Donnie accepted that they had just started on what we all agreed was Donnie's claim, resulting in his agreeing to let them keep the contents in the box. Wes and Randy want it noted that they did not know who was dredging and did not rat out any particular miners!

The lesson was not lost on any of us. We did not do it again because we did not give in to the temptation to mine on anyone else's claim again. At least, I didn't. Guess I can't speak for anyone else. In this way, we avoided one of the vices of gold mining.

Gold brings out envy (if you are getting gold, we want to be where you are!) and greed in people. Remember *Treasure of the Sierra Madre?* Real life gold mining, the model for that movie, can have similar motivation.

I had five claims beside the road with easy access to each one. These were the most hammered claims on the river because everyone driving past, especially the tourists to Alaska, thought along the lines Kurt, Rich and I had on Donnie's claim. One could make an argument for karma here.

Years later, I got one of those urges to visit the 40 Mile. When I arrived at my claims by the road, 12 people were panning and using high bankers, a type of mechanical sluice. When I alerted them to the error of their ways, they said, "We did not know." One is required by law to find out whether a piece of land is claimed and if so, by whom, then get permission from the claim owner before pursuing any kind of mineral extraction.

One day, also years later, in my store in Tok, which is 87 miles from the South Fork bridge, a distance that gives people a sense of having arrived in civilization from the wilds, a young Danish couple came in. They had tales of panning in the Klondike River in Dawson City, Yukon Territory, Canada, scene of the great Klondike gold rush. They were flushed with the excitement of their great panning bonanza. When I asked to see what they were going on about, they pulled out their vial of gold with a few flakes in water, handing it to me to look at. I encouraged them to finish their tale.

Besides paying to pan on a notorious creek in Dawson, they had stopped along the Taylor Highway and done more panning as they proceeded on their vacation itinerary. Knowing that my claims were the only ones by the road on that route, I asked for more details.

"Oh, we just went down to the river along the road and got more gold than we did in Dawson, and we didn't have to pay to pan it."

Still holding their vial, I said, "Those are my claims, so this gold belongs to me. Thanks for doing the hard work of panning it out of the river." I put it in my pocket.

Their mouths fell open, as they almost started crying. "We did not know."

"You are required by law to know or find out. People have been shot for this exact thing. Books have been written; movies have been made. It is called claim jumping. If you want to pan, you must stomp around in the brush until you find the claim location notice and contact the owner, who has paid fees to the State of Alaska to maintain the claims, done assessment work yearly, dealt with people like you coming along taking the irreplaceable gold off the claim, and has had dreams of getting that gold herself!"

During this whole speech, I had taken their vial out of my pocket and was rolling it in my hand. Crestfallen and disappointed, they could hardly take their eyes off of the vial. After a dramatic pause, during which I was remembering that this was my karma and knowing that panning for an hour or two on most claims doesn't remove enough gold to make any noticeable difference, I gave them back the gold, saying, "Gold is a strange thing. It can bring out the worst in people. Another person might not give it back to you because technically, it does not belong to you. People have been shot for this."

17. COFFEE TOSS, THEN VISITORS

Rich and whichever crew we were working with cooked their own breakfasts as they hung out waking up, talking and listening to the one radio station we got. The radio, powered by a car battery, had a wire for an antenna which was strung up between trees in the direction of the radio station. I did not usually go down and get in their way.

Once, in the summer of 1986 when I woke up energetic, I went down to the living room tent where they were listening to some talk radio thing I did not want to hear. As they were talking, not listening, I went outside to the staked ground for the radio and pulled the stake out, disabling the radio signal. Our world went silent.

"That's more like it," I thought, except for some reason, the hair on the back of my PMSin' neck was standing up.

Rich came out of the tent moving toward me aggressively. I was suddenly kind of nervous. He reached over and calmly took the brand-new Taster's Choice glass jar from my hands, set up into a classic shot-put stance, then launched (or "put" in track and field jargon) my coffee into the air. It seemed to hang there for a long time as it arced over the river until it crashed into the cliffs on the other side.

The shock and beauty of the whole episode was accompanied by the symphony of that Taster's Choice jar shattering into thousands of pieces. All right. I loved it. Though that was some valuable coffee due to having to go 200 miles round trip to replace it, the loss was almost worth it to see Rich execute his form from his award-winning shot put days in high school. It was the one and only time I got to see it in the 18 years I knew him. However, once I heard about his skill, I was one of his biggest shot put fans.

For at least 25 years, his shot put record was the longest standing track and field record at his high school and may still be, for all I know. He said his civics teacher once said to him, "Mr. Goodson, if you spent as much time on civics as you do thinking about track and field, you would be an 'A' student!" He told me he sat in class, thinking about how much more weight he had to lift to put the shot one more inch. He brought the same level of desire to be master of the shot put as he brought to gold mining.

I stood there for a moment, processing Rich's action, then went back to bed until the guys left.

On Tuesday, August 26, Rich took me upriver to vote in Chicken. Afterward, he went back down because the water had been so low on the upriver trip, he was afraid he could not get home if he waited any longer. Since we were expecting company on Friday, and not knowing whether the boat could get back up again, I hung out around Chicken. I slept in the truck until Gary and Kyle Gantz, father and son friends from Anchorage, showed up to spend five days on the river.

While waiting to meet up, they let their dog out of the van. She immediately disappeared. After five hours of their calling and looking for her, she was still gone when I got there. Gary decided to leave her running wild until he came back out in a few days. He did not see her again on his trip. When he got 400 miles back to Anchorage almost a week later, she was there! A tourist had picked her up on the Taylor Highway and used her tags to get her home.

We drove two miles along the river to the end of a really rough road so we could park as close as possible to our camp eight miles down. The parking put us six miles from camp. We were going to have to hike. While Gary distributed the load into my empty pack and the two packs they brought, Kyle and I took one last fruitless look for the dog. Then, we were on our way.

When we got down to Walker Fork gravel bar after two miles of hiking, they were getting worn out from carrying the packs. There was no trail, just tundra, cliffs, and rocky beaches. We dropped all the packs onto the gravel bar. Rich had told me he thought he could get that far up in the boat if they or their packs needed transporting.

Since I was in the peak years of my physical abilities, I wanted to go faster. After a mile, I told them to keep hiking, as I was going on ahead and would be back with the boat as soon as possible and pick them up. Then we would go back up to Walker Fork and get the packs. I told them to stop at Donnie Snyder's camp at mile six. They could not miss it since it was the only tent along the way.

I stopped in at Donnie's and asked him to give them some water or something when they got to his camp.

Down at our camp, I was across the river and yelled over to Rich, who came across in the boat and picked me up. We got up to Donnie's where we found Kyle and Gary. After getting the packs, we went back to camp. I asked them what was in the packs that made them so heavy. They said wait and see. Mysterious.

The next day Kyle and Gary went down to the dredge to watch the guys dredge and do some hiking and fishing for Arctic grayling, which I would say are the most abundant type of fish in this river. When they got back to camp, they said now we can tell you what is in the packs. They had brought steaks, potatoes, sour cream, butter, chives, vodka, and several bottles of wine—in addition to their camping gear and fishing tackle. No wonder we got tired when carrying those packs!

That night we had surf and turf! I put out our very best paper towels to use as napkins; we sat on lawn chairs with our paper plates in our laps. Oh, so festive! Visitors from the city. Sparkle in the day.

Kyle was 10 years old in 1986. Over the next eight years, he came back two more times.

L to R: Nicky, Kyle, and Janice

In 1991, Kyle came to the river with my nephew from Hawaii, Nick. They were 15 and 20 years old. Pretty adventurous of them to come so far from home. Nick wore his sweatshirt the whole time he was visiting. Alaska in the summertime is still colder than Hawaii at any time. Actually, I wore my sweatshirt most of the time too, as it keeps the chill, sun, and mosquitoes at bay.

They went to the dredge with Kurt and Rich, fishing and watching the dredgers and reading books in down time. They even saw a bear across the river. Since all this is so extraordinary to most people's experience, even riding in the truck on the rough and remote Taylor Highway as we drove to Tok to take them to the bus back to Anchorage was exciting.

In 1994 Kyle came up again, this time by himself. During this visit, I gave him driving lessons in my truck on the Chicken airstrip. It was as level and straight and traffic free as anything anywhere. I can still see that experience in my mind's eye. He would start at the end of the runway, accelerate with the gas pedal punched to the floor, then halfway, start braking to keep from hurtling off the end of the runway into the woods, while I tried to keep from stomping a hole in the floor on the passenger side. It turned out to be not so much driving training as a lesson in accelerating, braking, changing gears, and being in and out of control (there is a lot of that out here).

We swam in Mosquito Fork. He fished. He hiked with Rich and Rod Knight, to the summit of Mt. Fairplay, elevation 5,541 ft. At the top there is an incredible, expansive view of the Alaska Range in the distance and the uplands of the 40 Mile. The guys left my binoculars on a rock where they had sat, taking in the view and catching their breath.

Nobody was about to go back up that mountain to fetch the binoculars because, for one thing, there was no trail through a massive rock field, so they would have had a difficult time locating the exact rock they had sat on. I hope some hiker found the binoculars in time; one rainstorm might have done them in.

All in all, Kyle always fit right into the wilderness. To this day, he hikes the mountain trails overlooking Anchorage, hikes many newcomers are here to experience, though few do.

Nick came back more recently to Tok, too. This time his long-time partner, Jessie, came with him. Jessie did not like the Alaskan lifestyle I lived. It's not for everybody. They only stayed four days. I am pretty sure if their visit had been two weeks, I could have converted her!

18. EVELYN AND CHICKEN 1986

Tension rose inside me. The seeming confinement in the camp closed in all around. I made the decision to escape on foot. The river was too low to boat all the way up. Tomorrow, after the guys left for the long day of dredging, I would hike the one and a half miles up to Napoleon valley, after which I would hike the four miles over the saddle and across Walker Fork, ending with a steep climb up to the Taylor Highway, two miles from my truck. After an eight-mile drive, I would be in Chicken. I had no plan for getting home and no sleeping gear. I would cross that bridge when I came to it.

I spent the day preparing. I wrote letters I wanted to mail, and loaded my day pack with water, food, dry socks, "city" shoes, flashlight, toilet paper, Chapstick, and several layers of clothes, including a rain suit. I had decided not to tell the guys. When they came home, I went about my evening chores as usual. I could hardly believe no one sensed any undercurrent of intrigue.

The following morning passed in the same fashion with my being practically electrified and full of this sense of impending adventure. Still, no one noticed.

As soon as they left, I wrote a note saying I had gone to Chicken, not saying when I would return because I did not know. I grabbed my pack, and headed toward Napoleon, looking over my shoulder as I went. Surely, they were on to my plan and would catch me in the act before I rounded the first bend.

Each step was a step toward freedom. From what, though? We lived in the middle of nowhere; was it freedom from the freedom? Nothing so esoteric was my guess. I think the need to talk to another woman drove me on. Men not only don't talk about "girl" stuff, but they also don't particularly want to hear it either. Maybe some men, who weren't bothered by this, existed out there in the world somewhere, but they didn't live in our camp. I was on a quest to talk about knitting, recipes, and what dorks some men can be. I was willing to travel a long distance to do so.

Any time a person takes off into the Bush alone, a sense of self sufficiency kicks in, as well as an awareness of the ever-present threat of bears, for which Napoleon seems to be a magnet.

Halfway to Napoleon on the trail along the river, there is a rock outcropping with a single two-foot stretch with no hand or foot holds and nothing but river underneath it. A person has to press herself into the rock and advance with the faith her leading foot will find the little shelf at the end of the stretch; otherwise, it is into the deep eddy below because there is no going backward. If I fell in, my trip was over. I was all concentration, with a little bit of fear, as I approached this one bit of exposure. I was determined not to do any swimming. Full of confidence, I had less trouble than ever with it. Great start! The rest of the mile and a half was easy walking.

Today, my first goal was to get to Napoleon and hang out with Evelyn Soha, mother of 10 grown children. At that time, she was the only other woman in a gold camp anywhere on the almost 30 miles of South Fork, so I knew she would be glad to have me visit. When I arrived, she and her husband, Lou, were sitting down to breakfast and asked me to join them, which I accepted, giving in to the singular pleasure of having someone else cook and serve me breakfast. We passed a pleasant hour chatting. I almost gave in to the temptation to spend the day with her, but I had Chicken on my mind.

The next four miles were a test of my determination. I struggled up to the top of the saddle, an incline so steep trucks had difficulty getting up, particularly if it was wet for any reason. On top, I was thinking the worst was over, until I looked down into a swamp of some of the muddiest, deepest ruts one could imagine, the result of many trucks and other heavy equipment being stuck in this boggy, mile-long swamp. A bad situation had become worse.

Walking turned out to be a nightmare. To either side of the mud was swamp and hillocks. With every step, the mud tried to pull off my boot. So far, the trip out of Napoleon felt like basic training. Although much shorter in distance than walking the eight miles up the river, it was many times more difficult.

The next hurdle was Walker Fork. The water was just over my boots, so I walked across, sat down, emptied the water out and changed socks. The rest of the hike was uphill, with no defined trail. There were lots of minor trails, so I picked one and kept walking, hoping I did not have to backtrack because I was running out of steam.

Eventually, I came to the Taylor Highway, where I was certain someone would pick me up and take me the two miles down to my truck at South Fork bridge. But, after putting one heavy foot in front of the other long enough and stepping out of the way of the motorhomes and other traffic that zoomed past my outstretched thumb, I had walked all the way to my truck. Chicken was still eight miles away, and the day was half over. I felt like I had put in a full day already, but with my goal so close at hand, quitting was not an option. I changed clothes and went to town, refreshed, hoping the worst was over.

I spent the rest of the day talking to Lynne Burton, the postmaster and one of my best friends, until she closed at 5 p.m.

At this point, reality kicked in. I did not have a plan for getting home. I went down to the bar, where several South Fork dredgers were hanging out. After talking it over with two or three others, I convinced a dredger with a boat to take us all home.

We left the bridge area at 8 p.m., at a time in the year when darkness was falling. By the time we got two miles down, we were in complete darkness, traveling at a fast clip in a very shallow river, doing what the boat driver called skimming. Because his boat had so many holes in the bottom from this kind of boating in the past and the self-bailer could only do its job while going at a certain speed, the driver was convinced that if he went fast enough, he could go on top of the water and not hit rocks. We were into new territory in my boating experience. His theory came to an end when we encountered a big rock, which we could not see, sticking up out of the water. The boat came to an abrupt stop as it got high-centered. Everybody was violently thrown forward by the sudden stop. The driver told someone to get out and push us off the rock.

Since it was night and we still had miles to go, no one wanted to. We tried all kinds of creative ways to rock the boat loose without getting wet, without success. In the end, I got out and pushed us off.

I had never seen anybody drive a boat this way. In our camp we took it slow, so, in the event we did hit a rock, it would not cripple the boat. We had long wondered why the driver always pulled his boat up out of the water. Now we knew that if he did not pull it up, it would sink due to all the holes from hitting all those rocks. To this day, many rocks up and down the river have aluminum on them from the bottom of boats doing this kind of river running.

By the time I got home, six more miles downriver, I had had a full day. The guys in my camp loved hearing what was going on in town, amazed at what I had done. I never did it again, though. Sometimes, once is enough.

19. NORTH FORK 1988

Rich and I were camped and mining up the North Fork in the summer of 1988.

Joe, Gary and Clyde were at Ivan Creek on the South Fork. They had the gold wheel at their camp 20 miles away by river. Occasionally, Rich went down to use the wheel and enjoy some man talk.

One day when he went to the guys' camp, they were on the most gold we ever got in one hour: 3 ounces! That one day yielded 27 ounces. Rich decided to spend the night so he could participate. The next day they were back down to ounce an hour. This event was one of the highlights of our dredging careers.

When we left yesterday, the dredge was floating. This was the second consecutive day the river dropped overnight leaving the dredge high and dry. In order to work, we had to take the heavy dredge apart and reassemble it in the river. Extra work

While all that excitement was playing out on South Fork, up on the North Fork my job was to watch the river level. Two days before, we had come up to the dredging spot from camp to find the 8″ sitting high and dry on the gravel bar on the other side of the river from our camp and upriver a quarter mile. This was due to a rapidly dropping river. The dredge was grounded.

It was one thing for the dredge to be on the same side of the river as the camp; it was easier to keep an eye on and deal with. But being across the river added a layer of stress, especially since we didn't know how long Rich was going to be away with the boat. On the previous two days, we had to take the dredge apart to get it back in the river. We did not want to do that again, hence the importance of watching the river level rise and fall.

In mid-afternoon, I decided to deal with the dredge once and for all by staking it out in the river. The only river crossing vessel I had was little better than wading because it was hard to maneuver: the $30 one-person blowup raft, guided by a gold pan paddle.

Once I made it across the river, I was in no hurry to go back. I kept hoping Rich would come back before I had to get back in the raft. It seemed to have a mind of its own!

When I finished securing the dredge, I was wet from wading out into the river. Getting into the raft had lost its threat. I was already wet.

I did several visual checks throughout the rest of the day. Rich was home before any decision to repeat had to be made.

I stayed there for two months. Rich and I were the only people on the North Fork. I did not see anyone but Rich. I have always been a homebody and being on the river was no exception. Most of the time, I was content to hold down the fort while the other members of our various camps came and went. When I went to Chicken at the end of that summer, Lynne Burton told me she was glad to see me after all that time. She had wondered whether anything untoward had happened to me.

Rich and I got 100 ozt that summer, and in September, after his two coworkers left for the season, Gary came up and worked with Rich. I became the camp person. They also recovered 100 ozt in that great spot.

20. A Year to Remember 1989

1989 was a high point. It was the first year of the video camera, allowing us to document every aspect of dredging. As is often the case when a person gets a new camera, we carried it everywhere we went. Although it interfered with the natural flow of our lives, we had actual video of what went on day to day. The documenting of our lives on video allowed me to step back and see our mining lives from a different perspective. I still watch these videos and go back visually and audibly to one of our best years, a year that everything fell into place.

Both dredges were on the North Fork. Rich and I were on the 8" dredge, prospecting down the river from the Kink, popping holes for six miles, looking for another hot spot in the 24 claims. We moved camp frequently as we moved the dredge further down. Camp was bare bones but comfy. We even had CB radio connection with Gary, Joe and Clyde, three miles downriver from us at Hilda Creek on the 10" dredge.

This was also one of the big gold years. Our total was 540 ounces. This was not an overnight thing. It took us 10 years to get to this point.

The diver with Joe Taylor tending.

1989 was also a low point, though I did not know it at the time. It was the year Rich got into the stock market, which absorbed his attention as completely as the gold mining did. I thought it was a good thing, even when he set the alarm for 3:30 a.m. to watch some business show on television when we were in town in the winter. I did not know yet that one could gamble in the market.

We hardly saw anyone else that summer. The Bureau of Land Management (BLM) group floated through in early August, and at the end of the season a couple of rafts of caribou hunters floated through together. The BLM group had a woman, Holly, in it, so yay, she and I made our own little group, while the guys hung out together. Two or three days after they visited, I got very sick with the flu, while the guys did not.

When we were finally off the river for good and back in Chicken, I went to the post office and asked if Holly had recovered from her bout with the flu. I was assured she had.

"Great," I said. "She gave me the flu out in the middle of nowhere. I want to be the one to kill her, as that flu almost did to me."

In keeping with the general goodness of this year, this was a bumper crop year for the wild raspberries. Once they started getting ripe in mid-July, they came on day after day until August 23. Nearly every morning, I would eat as many as I wanted, and the next day, I could do it again.

In August, we started running low on gas. With the river at an extreme low point, hauling in enough gas for the rest of the season was going to be problematic.

Plan A. Rich and Gary decided to make the run carrying nothing but two empty barrels. The plan was to get more barrels from our stash upriver. They had a terrible time getting the almost empty boat up to the landing, having to jump out to pull the boat over rocks sticking up out of the water in the many low places. There was no way they could take any full barrels back to camp in the boat.

Plan B. They went to Tok to check on a helicopter to carry full barrels from the Chicken airport, over the mountains, to our camp on the North Fork. This was a journey 50 miles by Taylor Highway and boat, down a river almost out of water, but only 19 miles by air as the raven flies.

The Tok helicopter service was unavailable. Rich and Gary found a service in Fairbanks which would do it, two barrels at a time. The helicopter was new. The pilot did not know how the barrels, suspended by a cable, would fly, but since he was Alaskan, he was up for adventure, 300 road miles from home base.

While Gary and Rich were filling up the barrels at the gas station at Susan Wiren's, they were talking to local miners, who took an interest and started drifting down to the airport to watch this rare event go down. At the beginning, two or three miners were there helping.

After the first lift off and flying in a direction aircraft did not usually fly, then another trip 15 minutes later, people from the bar and post office gathered at the airport. An impromptu party formed around the loading of the barrels and the 10 trips of taking 19 barrels at 15 minutes a trip or a total of two and a half hours. During that time, at least one miner worked out a deal with the pilot and had his gas carried in this easy way.

This was before helicopters and small planes became commonplace around Chicken as a result of increased interest in mineral exploration. Chicken airport was a super convenient staging point. After exploration began, all the comings and goings were hardly noticed, certainly not occasions to go down to the airport and hang out for an afternoon.

Clyde, Joe, and I were at the camp receiving all that gas via air delivery, gas which had so recently been in town. All this summer we had been feeling so isolated. We were made aware how close to town we were, if only we had a helicopter!

By this means, we were able to get enough gas to finish the season.

Then, if that was not enough, when we got back to Chicken at the end of the season, we encountered our friend, Mike O'Gorman. This meeting resulted in our buying his cabin and the two claims associated with it, three and a half miles from Chicken. In an area where private land was rarely available, this made our lives so much more bearable. At last, we had a place to leave equipment over the winter, as well as a place to stay, and icing on the cake, we even two claims to prospect.

Kurt Houser, left, and Randy Raffety, a fellow dredger on the right, in front of the cabin.

Another plus in 1989: I met Ariadne (Ari) Wiren and her son, Greg and his wife Susan, when they bought Beautiful Downtown Chicken. Ari had just retired from a career in finance in Philadelphia and became an unlikely resident of Chicken, as well as my running buddy for the next 17 years.

Her father had been killed by the Bolsheviks in the Russian revolution. At that time wealthy families were considered allies of the Czar. The family lived in St Petersburg and were wealthy landowners. Among their landholdings was land in northern Russia. Ari's pregnant mother fled to there and finally found passage on a ship sailing from Archangel in the Arctic to London.

The ship encountered a storm on the way and was wrecked along the coast of England. The trauma caused her to give birth to Ari in a lifeboat plying its way to shore. Ari's place of birth is recorded as Liverpool, the closest town at the time! Mother and daughter soon immigrated first to Texas, then later to Philadelphia when Ari's mother married the man Ari knew as her father. Ari graduated from Drexel University in Philadelphia.

Greg and Susan spent some winters in Chicken, running and breeding sled dogs, hanging out with the other locals who wintered there.

I remember a picture of Susan bringing the kids up to Kurt's for trick-or-treat. Their costumes were sheets thrown over their heads making them scary ghosts, while underneath they wore heavy winter clothes. Then, for many years, they spent their winters in the Caribbean on his sailboat (so yes, they lived my original dream!), flying down in their own airplane.

What a year!

Ari Wiren on the left. Going right is Jerry, Greg Wiren, Susan Wiren, and Otis. The two non-Wirens are butchers from Fairbanks who came to visit in Chicken, bringing ribs from town!

21. Animals in 40 Mile Country

Though we did not see many other people during these summers, we were part of the summertime life cycles of animals living out there. Here are a few remembrances:

Grouse

From early summer 1986, our river family included a family of grouse: the red-adorned cock, the brown, gray, and white speckled hen, and the three babies. The birds have feathered legs. Lost feathers look and feel like clouds, having thick down on the end closest to the body with a smaller down feather attached so it covers the quill of the main feather. Other animals or birds line their nests with these soft feathers.

When we humans used the outhouse, which was open and away from camp, we were often checked out by curious grouse. They paraded around fearlessly while watching us watching them. They would roll in the dirt around the outhouse, looking like bathers in a dry birdbath, dirt and ruffled feathers all aflutter.

As we left for the winter, I told the grouse we were leaving and that we had enjoyed their companionship during the summer. I felt they were going to miss us, not understanding when we did not return.

Weasel

Cute and entertaining, the weasel is deceptive. It is a killing machine but not a predator of humans. The brown and white fur on its hot dog-shaped and -sized body, looked soft and felt softer, turning white in winter, at which time it is called an ermine. Its black, beady eyes watched, with intelligence, every movement within its range of vision. It darted from point to point, like a sprinter, pausing long enough to see somewhere else to run. They were around our camps and seemed to enjoy us.

At one of our camps in the summer of 1989, Rich and I had a weasel hanging around. I was cooking salmon from a can one day and put the can down to use both hands for something. When I looked around for the can, it was gone. After looking all the usual places, I noticed a two-inch opening under our plywood food storage box. Since I had looked everywhere else, I stuck my hand underneath, and there the salmon can was. I pulled it out with the weasel attached! It was so cute, I let the weasel have it and may have even added a bit of salmon back to the can.

Another time, we were up at the cabin, which had an underflooring. I saw a weasel pick up a screaming leveret (baby hare) and carry it off under the house. I could hear the weasel trying to jump up into the space between floors, with the hare in its mouth. For a long time, I heard that leveret being tortured by the weasel. I thought, quit playing with your food.

Mosquitoes

Mosquitoes make us aware of how awesome our bodies are. When something so tiny lands on us, our nerve endings alert us. We can feel them walking on the surface of our skin. How can something so tiny drive us so insane?

Moose

I had a container garden with 12 big containers of various vegetables, which I took particular pleasure in nurturing. All was well until one day we came back from dredging, and I went up to check to see how much the plants had grown while I was gone. To my horror, there was not one green thing left. A moose had come and eaten every plant down to the potting soil. Gone were the broccoli, peas, and lettuce. My heart was broken. I was so sad.

I said to any moose listening, "You could have left me something, anything." You are probably thinking, "How did you know it was a moose?" Moose nuggets were left as evidence.

Squirrel

When we left for town, we put all edibles in a 32-gallon garbage can and snapped the top on. The first thing we noticed when we got back and walked into camp was the lid, off the garbage can, on the other side of the camp. Something had chewed the edge most of the way around and gotten it off. When we examined the contents of the garbage can, nothing looked out of place.

Later, when we looked for the peanut butter jar, it was not in the garbage can where we kept it. One of us backed up and looked around.

The jar of peanut butter was on a branch of a huge spruce tree. The tree's base was 20 feet below us down beside the river, with the jar at our eye level. As we took back the jar, we left a smudge of peanut butter on the branch for the squirrel which had worked so hard for the reward.

Every year about the same time, squirrels dropped spruce cones on the tent roof making splat noises, as though heavy raindrops were hitting the plastic. All over the forest, squirrels were harvesting the newest cones from the spruce treetops and tossing them onto the forest floor. Later they would gather up the spruce cones and stash them for winter consumption.

Peregrine Falcon and Red-necked Grebe

In the summer of 1988 Rich and I camped at Wilson Creek on the North Fork and dredged a mile upriver. As we boated up to the claim, we came around a corner in time to see an adult peregrine falcon in a stoop, which is a nosedive which can reach 200 mph, with a 10G turn at the bottom. According to those who know, the falcon's stoop would knock out a human. The brute force of the hit on most targets kills, right then and there.

What Rich and I happened upon was this: The fastest animal on the planet, the peerless peregrine, was matching wits with a red-necked grebe, a medium-size, aquatic, diving bird, the size the peregrine loves the most and part bird, part submarine. As this drama played out before us, we noticed that the falcon's youngster at the top of a spruce tree was watching the parent falcon's hunting technique.

The mother grebe was leading her eight chicks on a float trip when the falcon threat commenced. She was aware of the looming threat and kept the youngsters close to the shore where there were lots of rocks offering protection both camouflage and physical, as who wants to dive into a pile of rocks! She apparently told them to stay there because they bobbed in place close to the river rocks, as she went back to the river. She swam out into the middle, leading the falcon away from her babies. When the falcon started its stoop, she ducked underwater where she stayed until the threat was over. Falcons can only do this maneuver once or twice because it takes an enormous amount of energy.

Some days later, we saw the mother grebe with her chicks again. This time there were only six.

If you have ever seen a grebe flying over the top of the water, you might have made note of its low altitude flying, just above the surface of the water. If they can get underwater before the falcon gets them, they stand a chance. If not, the falcon is going to outfly them and knock them cuckoo.

Golden Eagle

1989. Rich and I were in the boat speeding downriver on a long lake area, when an eagle appeared 10 feet above and in front of us, flying downriver also, wings spread out six feet, matching our speed and looking down at us. Glorious. Amazing how large they are! Still resonates after 30 years.

Bald Eagle

I was working outside when I felt an intrusion into my space, although no one was around. I looked up and ahead to see a bald eagle, 20 feet above, gliding toward me, riding the air current. The only noise this gigantic bird made was the sound of its feathers rubbing against each other, as it adjusted wings in the air. It looked me in the eye as it floated closer. We had a moment of connection. Then, it glided by.

What we saw:
Golden and bald eagles, peregrines, owls, ravens, chickadees, juncos, robins, gray jays, magpies, grebes, swallows, and even seagulls(!). Bears, wolves, foxes, lynx, coyotes, moose, and caribou. Marmots, squirrels, hares, martins, weasels, grouse, ptarmigan, porcupines, and voles. I have heard there are wolverines but have never seen one. Butterflies, grasshoppers, and dragonflies. Frogs, mosquitoes, no-see-ums, horseflies, black beetles with claws, yellow jackets, hornets, wasps, and spiders. (I love lists.)

This is a partial list of animals in the 40 Mile area. The area is remote. At first, the space looks empty, but many species live out there. Year after year, we observed their realities as their neighbors. My point is: We were not alone…

22. MUSINGS

Leaves were beginning to turn. Around September 10, they would be gone in our short and early autumn. More often, the air temperature was warm, the wind temperature cold. Darkness came a bit earlier now, so we had a chance to see the auroras, free for the looking, the ultimate light show.

Already late autumn. August 25, 2001

Today is August 25, 2001. I put on my long john bottoms for the first time this season. I felt the extra restrictive layer, knowing the knit would relax, expand, and disappear into the clothing covering my now winter-clad body. The main thing about this new layer was when I pulled my pants down to potty, I would have to remember to pull up three layers instead of two. The first few times I pottied after putting the bottoms on, I pulled my garments back up, then noticed a wad of material, which turned out to be a forgotten layer, still down while the other two were up!

I had on my polar fleece jacket and my Mackinac Island Michigan sweatshirt and sweatpants. I also had three logs cranking in the wood stove, doing the chill chasing in this 20' x 16' room. I'd had a small fire constantly for two or three days, giving me awareness that things were changing. I also noticed the geese flying south, squawking back and forth to each other. I wondered what they were saying. They reminded me of chores to be done before the snow and cold came. Migrating geese are not to be ignored.

Yesterday, in early September 1992, I drove from Anchorage to Chicken, more of a change than the 409 miles NE might seem to indicate. The air here was colder, the trees mostly yellow. Silence reigned, broken by occasional faraway, man-made noise of bulldozers working somewhere down the valley, as well as the "caw" of a raven or the chatter of a squirrel, as I invaded its perceived territory (Hey, I live here too!).

Noise also resulted from the breeze in the trees, causing the leaves to flutter on their stems, rustling with different sounds, depending on how many leaves were involved and what shade of green or gold they were. Every now and then, the wind blew so hard the air became full of leaves, churning around on currents of air and looking for a moment like snow.

The aspens shimmered in front of the eye and ear. Leaf color at its peak. Sun behind golden trees dazzles the eye. Most falling leaves yet. The next day, all that was left was the skeletons of yesterday's dazzlers and a carpet of yellow on the ground, the roof, and the wash water in the tub.

Today, as I routinely moved around the cabin, a new element made itself known, one I was expecting but not ready for. The first snow. I bent over to adjust the wood stove. When I straightened up, I was facing the window where two hours ago, the leafless aspens stood like skeletons. They now sported lines of snow on every twig, on every tree—very complex, very white—until the snow melted, or the wind or weight of the pile cleared the branches. The ground had turned white.

I was spending the winter in Anchorage. We were enjoying temperatures around +30. I went to Tok, 325 miles NE, for Christmas. January 1-4, the temperature was -60°F. The day I left to return to Anchorage, I drove for an hour at -40°F through extremely remote Alaska, where the highway cuts through mountain ranges, then into a more southerly river valley for three hours at -10°F, then two hours at sea level at +20°F. This is one reason I like Anchorage in the winter. On the same day, three areas had a temperature difference of 60 degrees. Being more southerly, Anchorage is almost balmy by comparison.

On the drive down, I could not allow myself to think about car breakdown. Minus forty degrees F is very hard on vehicles. Everything plastic can crack and break. When I sat on the vinyl seat of the car before it was warmed up, the seat cracked. The plastic cables inside the door that operated the door handles snapped.

Just going for Christmas was a survival trip. We always knew it could be. This was Alaska in coldest, darkest winter.

23. 1991, 1992

1991: As we boated up and down moving our gear between camp and the bridge, we saw an unknown dredger setting up his mining operation two miles down the Mainstem from the 40 Mile bridge. He differed from most miners in that he did not have a boat. Instead, he was transferring his equipment either on his back or by floating some of it in a $30 one-person raft. I already liked him, as I had one of those rafts too. As we boated by several times, I gained respect for him doing this the harder way. At some point, we stopped and talked, and Rudd Van Dyne came into our lives. He was and is a dredger who loved gold the way we do. He's one of my best friends. His prospecting and production skills are legendary.

Me and Rudd van Dyne and a hovercraft on a trailer.

1992: Once again we prospected the Mainstem at the Smith Creek and Flat Creek areas, before moving down to the Claghorn Rapids area. Late in the season, we moved up to Burnt Bar above the bridge to the production site, where we put our dredge in beside the other 8″ dredge.

Kurt and Rich were on one, Gary and I on the other. For once, the prospecting dredge was in the money.

Winter came super early that year, the earliest I remember. By September 5th snow was falling. We worked in the increasingly cold, snowy days. Each day we expected the weather to change. It did not. On the 10th, we decided to call it quits when we woke up to slush going down the river. After packing up in a hurry, we took off in the boat. The slush was plugging up the jet foot resulting in the engine not getting the water it needed to cool down and generate power. By the time we got a mile down, we were at the top of the falls. I asked to be put out on shore so I could hand carry the gold in case something went amiss.

When I got to the bottom of the falls, Rich pulled the boat into the eddy on the right which was covered by a sheet of ice of unknown thickness. Rich told Kurt to get out and pull the boat to shore. Immediately, Kurt broke through the ice, getting completely wet and cold. He struggled to get through the ice to shore before hypothermia set in. Rich was already looking for Kurt's dry clothes by the time the boat was tied off. Kurt changed quickly, but he was shivering for an hour. They had made it safely through the falls only to encounter life threatening mishap at the bottom. That night, the temp plunged to -20°F! There was no Indian summer that year.

Our prospecting during both these summers did not turn up any new hot spots. Instead, those two summers turned out to be exercises in moving camp and equipment around, mainly resulting in weight training. We did cover our expenses when we moved up to the area with the production dredge.

24. Doogie Gets into Trouble

Here's how yesterday (summer 1992) went:

On Thursday afternoon, Kurt and Rich went to Chicken, 70 miles away—50 by road, 20 by boat—where they spent the night, leaving me and Doogie Houser without a boat, and five or six miles from our nearest neighbor. I am not a dog authority by any means, but I was pretty sure I could handle one night of being the Pack Leader.

Before Kurt and Rich left, they told me about the bear that had hung out in the bushes by the dredge three miles from here, keeping Doogie agitated on Wednesday. When they went to the dredge Thursday morning, the plastic gas tank on the shore had been ruptured by bear teeth or claws, so no dredging could be done until they got one from the cabin. The only thing to do was to go to Chicken.

Things went peacefully enough after they left, although Doogie was antsy all day. He kept looking toward the woods, barking, with the fur on his back standing up.

Doogie took over the recliner in the cabin next to the woodstove.

At 1 a.m., Doogie, tied down by the kitchen tent, began barking with authority and generally indicating that "something" was out there. I jumped out of bed and stuck my bare feet into rubber boots without pads (translated "COLD"), grabbed the shotgun, and took off in my long johns and T-shirt out into the 40°F darkness.

By the time I got to the kitchen, I had switched into the panic mode: Bears love kitchens. No bear was there, but it did not mean that in the next second, one would not charge out of the woods. I untied Doogie, so I would not shoot him accidentally, while trying to kill the bear that was trying to eat our "bear bait" dog.

When free, the first thing Doogie did was run off barking. I was beginning to realize I did not have enough clothes on but had no time to change that. I settled for calling the dog and whistling, which had worked in the past. Eventually he came back without my having heard any scuffle or yelping, and without a varmint on his trail. We were looking good at this point.

Standing there in the darkness, I noticed Doogie was smacking his lips, resulting in a clacking sound. Where had I heard that before? Oh dear. Porcupine quills. At least, it was not a bear. What did I know about quills? Not much. I thought I might need pliers to remove them; and maybe they should be pushed through, not pulled out, a less painful way to remove them. Quills that are left in can cause a fatal infection.

Some of the things I did not know were: Do porcupines get rabies? and How do people hold a flashlight in their mouths, pliers in one hand, a squirming dog in the other, and get the job done? Answers would have been helpful, but I had never asked the questions.

Now, I was in the middle of the night, shivering in the wilderness, responsible for emergency medical treatment and alone. Never having seen the procedure was a bit of a drawback. For instance, how does one push out a quill lodged in the nose which looked like an arrow in the center of a target? Where did the quill come out—the roof of the mouth or somewhere else? That sounded harder to deal with than pulling it out. His poor nose bled a lot from the three quills I extracted later.

I could not find pliers, so I tried using tweezers. Doogie did not like them because I could not get a good grip on the quill. I really could not see clearly and was freezing, so at 2:30 a.m., I decided to wait until sunrise, warming up in bed, and let Doogie live with it. Maybe he would be more cooperative after living with three quills in his nose, one under his muzzle, and nine in his lower lip.

I did not sleep. I put on a down vest, long sleeve shirt, wool jacket, wool pants and long johns, and wool socks. I got under three sleeping bags. It took me three hours to get warm.

During this time, the dog was whimpering. I was bothered by his misery and also by the knowledge that predators can hear wounded animals, and might come to camp, and attack the dog. Then, the stress of the porcupine on both of us would have been for nothing. I was ready with the shotgun but still so cold for most of the time, I was not certain I could hold it steady enough to shoot straight. Lee Fuel used to say he'd rather have a man point a gun at him than a woman because the woman might accidentally kill him. I put the gun in a corner and stepped around it until I warmed up.

At 5:34 a.m. there was finally enough light, and I was finally warm enough to have a new look at the situation. I remembered the Leatherman, the well-known multitool, found it, and was ready for action. Doogie was ready too. He was very brave, not crying, letting me pull seven quills—three from his nose, one under his chin, and three from one side of his bottom lip, leaving six quills in his lower lip. I did not try pushing them through, just went for it. That was all he could take, so we took a break from it. At 8:30 a.m., he let me pull one more from his lip, and that was it.

We had a long day of droopy dog and human. Neither one of us had had any sleep, and we weren't getting any during the down period, either. He could not sleep due to the quills because when he put his face forward on the ground, he would wake up after a few seconds' sleep, as the quills contacted the ground. He also could not take any more extractions, being very tired with his mouth hurting.

Me? I could hardly stand this usually smart, cute dog's pain. My stomach was in knots. How long did it take for the quills to fester and kill? I could not trick him into allowing me to pull out even one more. All I needed was one more pair of hands to hold him while I pulled the rest of them out. It would have been so simple that way.

Doogie began working on them himself. It broke my heart. I called out into the universe to Kurt and Rich or anyone else to come to the rescue. Around 2 p.m., the dog began to show signs of going crazy from lack of sleep since 1 a.m., six quills in his lips, and the wounds from the others, which harbored who-knows-what-kinds of pathogenic bacteria. It was all too much. Many times during the day, Doogie's eyes got that wanting-to-be-asleep but forced-to-be-awake, hurt and pained look that I totally understood. I was all too aware of every minute. Once or twice, I thought maybe it would have been better for both of us to have been eaten by the imaginary bear.

Sleep deprived, I listened for Rich and Kurt's return, straining my ears for the sound of a boat motor in the distance but hearing only silence. The hours passed slowly; the darkness crept in until it filled the world.

When the guys got back, they could not see to take out the remaining quills and left them for daylight. By this time, Doogie and I had been up for 21 hours, with only three hours of troubled rest the night before.

Kurt and Rich had no trouble getting the rest of the job done the next morning. The area around the quills had festered, and there was no fight left in Doogie. Also, there were two of them, that extra pair of hands I had needed.

Some dogs learn to avoid porcupines after one encounter. This dog did not. He went on to get into trouble two more times. One of those times was no big deal, but the third time was the big daddy of them all. That time he had so many quills, with several in his mouth where anesthesia is usually required for removal. He was crazed from the start.

Kurt had a 1952 mushing magazine, with a cover story on what to do in these cases. The main gist was to anesthetize the dog with whiskey, which we did not have. The three of us could not hold him down. We did manage to throw him in the boat and take him to the bar in Chicken, where we bought a pint of the cheapest whiskey they had. A group of guys held Doogie down and managed to pour half of that bottle into him, after which he settled down and allowed the removal of the quills.

For 24 hours, he was tied to the back bumper of a pickup truck, with a dazed look in his eyes. I am certain he was drunk; he sure smelled like it. Later, I thought he had a hangover. He must have learned a lesson through that experience. He never got in a porcupine's way again.

Once you see a dog with quills in its face, you never forget the sight, and you don't want to see it ever again!

25. MIDLIFE CRISIS & ARI'S CABIN

The 1993 mining season began with a bang. Rich had a midlife crisis, ran Kurt off, then ran off himself, coming and going all summer to our camp at Long Bar. Doogie and I were holding down the fort. We did no dredging that summer until late in the season, when both Kurt and Rich came back for the push to the end. Joe, Gary and Clyde worked on the other dredge upriver, as dependable as ever. We got a percentage from that dredge, making up for our own lack of dredging.

In July Rich gave me a birthday card saying he loved me, darlin.' In October he told me that he had gambled away our money.

At the end of the summer, we all returned to the cabin in Chicken. Rich then went on to Fairbanks with the guys, leaving Kurt and me in Chicken.

We were helping Ari, who had bought a cabin kit from a business in Tok. Ari's son, Greg, found carpenters from the mining community to help him get the logs up and roof on by early September. Then they all left, including Greg, leaving the windowless, empty cabin.

Ari found a carpenter in Delta Junction, 170 miles away, who agreed to spend time helping her, while also doing his own projects at home in Delta before winter came. Kurt also donated time to this project. I told Ari I would stay around until she was moved in, but I was no carpenter.

She and I made many runs to Fairbanks for kitchen cabinets, appliances, doors, flooring, lighting fixtures, windows, and whatever else the carpenter put on his long lists. We also got groceries and dog food and straw for the doghouses. Just as important, we also arranged for delivery, before the road closed, of enough propane for lights and kitchen stove, as well as fuel oil for the oil dripper heater to last through the long winter.

We moved the last box into the cabin October 31, the day of the first snow. That year, snow and cold were late, giving us just the right amount of warmth and no snow. The year before, freezing temps began September 11 and did not warm up. No Indian Summer. No mercy. But that was not the story this year. Mercy abounded for six or seven weeks in the autumn of 1993, while we four finished her beautiful cabin.

For the first time since she arrived five years before, she had her own home. As we carried in the boxes, I told Ari I was leaving. She had all winter to unpack and get settled in. I knew I was leaving her in a secure, warm house. I drove out of Chicken without guilt in a raging snowstorm.

26. BEAR EVENTS

Alaska in the Bush. The stuff dreams are made of. No ticks, no chiggers, no snakes. Mild temperatures. Pure air. Plenty of quiet time for inner focus. Nature unspoiled. And once you leave the few metropolitan areas, it is awesome in its size and the distances between outposts or even houses.

Out where we were, miles down a river with other dredge camps miles from here, still many miles from Chicken, which itself is isolated (no phones, few people, and one time a week mail delivery to the post office in those days), the quiet is broken by known noises—wind in the trees, squirrel chatter, one tree rubbing against another, times 101 comforting noises.

Always underneath the joy and freedom lurk the threat that the noise might be a bear—breaking branches, vocal grunts and growls, or the sound of the kitchen being turned upside down during a rainstorm at 2:45 a.m., the darkest part of the night, by more than one, grunting at each other. In this case, three crashed around in the kitchen! These noises stand apart from all the rest. They signal adrenaline-pumping, fight-or-flight, nitty gritty survival reactions and generate the kind of anxiety that takes years off one's life.

Other times, their smell preceded them!

June 1, 1980

Lee killed a bear with one shot when we had been in camp less than 24 hours. Carole and I were rookies to the outdoors. We had heard scary stories during our week up at the landing where almost everyone including the women were wearing pistols to walk from tent to tent or carrying rifles to the outhouse. We were on edge.

I was going toward the back of the tent outside and heard branches cracking behind. Knowing that Carole and Lee were down the hill, I wondered what could be making the noises, which sounded too big to be a squirrel, the only animal I was familiar with out here. Naturally, I stepped around the back corner of the tent. What I saw going around the other back corner was the rear end of a very big brown dog; at least, that's what my frame of reference called it.

Where did that dog come from? Slowly, it dawned on me, this was no dog. I drew back, trying to remember what Carole and I had practiced earlier. Panic seemed most appropriate, so I hollered, "Bear. Bear. Bear," spaced what seemed eons apart, and during the seemingly interminable interval, waiting for Lee to react to my warnings, I decided to run from the tent on the side where I was and down the hill, across the rocky beach, and into the water, putting myself behind Lee. When I was certain Lee had the gun, I put my plan into action, making a speeding bullet seem slow. Later, I looked at the thick bushes I had run through and wondered how I got through without tearing myself to pieces.

I was on my way down the hill when I heard the shot. The bear did not know what hit him. He fell in a close area, between the tent and a tree. He had been standing on his hind legs to make himself look larger. Strangely enough, there was not a drop of blood on the tent.

Carole and I were Lee's second shadow for a few days, after which I sorta relaxed, especially after hearing from people in camps upriver that they actually had not seen bears in two years. Somewhere in this time frame, Carole left, so there were fewer targets if a bear did arrive again.

Eight days later, I was sleeping in the middle of Lee's tent – I had not yet summoned the courage to sleep in my own tent again – and Lee was next to the side of the tent where the bear had fallen, when something woke me up. Lee had sat up and was rubbing his eyes to wake himself up. He grabbed the gun, and reaching over, put his hand over my mouth, whispering, "Bear. Shh."

This time, a bear had come up the beach, past the bear hide drying there and walked up the hill and around the tent to the place where the other bear had died. Lee awoke when something nudged his arm through the tent. We could see the bear's nose through the nylon, as it touched the tightly stretched tent, following Lee's arm from hand upward to where the bear attempted to bite Lee's shoulder. When Lee sat up, the bear left, probably thinking the tent was a living thing, but what exactly? And why did it just walk away without tearing the tent apart to find out?

We were able to see from this bear's footprints that it had earlier circled the hide on the beach and our tent while we slept on.

Over the years since, people in all walks of life have wanted to discuss that first bear with us. They asked whether we could have run it off and spared its life. I have thought long and hard about this. It came along on our first day out there. After the week upriver with everyone stirring up the fear, there simply was not enough time to consider options. The bear came into our camp and into our midst. Further experience in bear country led us to understand that their curiosity would cause them to come back again and again.

We never killed another bear in our camps. We learned more as we lived among them. There are some bears that won't be run off. It's a showdown. Handguns are not ideal for shooting bears. Once a bear is a garbage bear, it is likely always a garbage bear. It will be back. They are curious. Bears don't have anywhere else to be, thus have more time on their paws for opening every package of beans stored in a 32-gallon garbage can.

1985

Before we got to our camp where we had stashed mining supplies over the winter, the bears did. A Coleman ice chest, containing cans of salmon and grains in plastic bags, was totally trashed. The cans were not opened; the bags of grains were. A one-gallon can of Blazo white gas was punctured with the ripping claw-mark signature, as was a one-gallon container of Thompson's Water Seal. Why the bear preferred the chemicals, we did not know. We suspected that this was going to be a summer of socializing with the normally antisocial prince of the wilderness. How wrong our premonitions were. Even though the physical damage done was small, the mental toll was enormous.

The black bear is smaller than the grizzly, and while not known for being as fierce, it can wreak its own brand of havoc on things physical and mental. Since they are pretty much without predators, they grow into an attitude of having things their own way. There are few barriers that will keep them out for long. Added to their unpredictability is the curious nature that creates so much destruction, as well as fear in humans. A bear went through our camp several times that summer, never doing much but always doing something that left us uneasy.

At one point before we had our outhouse hole dug – the permafrost slowed digging – all three members of our camp had individual spots where we went potty. One day, each of us found a territorial pile of bear scat (scientific/polite way to say poop) on top of our human pile.

July 1987

We took a 32-gallon plastic garbage can full of one-pound packages of dried beans and rice and two boxes of crackers in our first load to a new camp. When we came back with another load three days later, the garbage can was full of claw marks, knocked over, and almost empty. Beans of many colors were everywhere; there were green peas, lentils, pintos, kidney beans, black beans, great northern beans, small red beans, lima beans, azuki beans and garbanzos. They were ankle deep in many places. In other places, they had been there long enough to start mildewing or sprouting. Every package had been torn open and the contents scattered. The two cracker boxes lay empty in the midst of it all. After the initial shock subsided a bit, I lapsed into a Zen-like mode and began picking up the thousands of beans. Since the floor was mostly dirt, cleaning up this mess was a new experience; it gave new meaning to wilderness living. When I tried shoveling the plywood portion of the floor, most of the beans fell off onto the dirt. So, I wound up using a broom and dustpan on the wood floor and picking up most of the beans in the dirt and tundra with my fingers. Quite the chore, but when it was finally done, I felt very satisfied and pretty certain I didn't want to do that again.

Same summer, same camp

July 29: The foam dredge pontoons were pulled up on the bank. We found claw marks in the foam, and a neoprene glove and hood Rich used had chunks chewed out. While we were at the dredge, 1 p.m. to 7:30 p.m., a bear or bears went into camp and made a massive mess in the kitchen. Among other things, they had eaten my birthday salmon filet, dropped off on the kitchen counter by another dredger that day while we gone, as well as Rich's candy bars. That paper with the delicious smell where the salmon had been and the candy bar wrappers were all that was left. Oh yes, and some crumbs of cornbread.

July 30: At 2:45 a.m., through the pouring rain, we heard grunts and crashes in the kitchen. Rich got up with the gun and told me to stay in our sleeping tent. I said "No. You might shoot me. I'm going to be right behind you!" There were two young bears in our kitchen and a mama bear out in the thick alder bushes around camp. He shot the gun above them and scared them off.

At 4:30 a.m., the rain had stopped. We could hear clearly when the three bears returned. This time we ran down, yelling like banshees and scared them off. As they ran down our trail to the river, Rich shot over their heads.

In the daylight, we went dredging. One of my jobs was to get enough gas for the day. As I approached the barrel, I could smell gas. It turned out that Rich had shot a hole in the top of the barrel! We siphoned the gas to another barrel. When the first barrel was empty, I recovered the slug, which I still have to this day. It is one of my treasures. Rich, the great barrel hunter.

July 31: We were down at the river panning down the day's concentrates and saw the bears on the cliffs across the river.

August 1: We were down at the river panning again and heard ducks floating down. When we looked, our ducks turned out to be the three bears floating along with the current in the river, speaking some kind of conversation that sounded like squawking. The mother and the brother got out before the cliffs when they caught our scent. The sister missed her chance and went floating by us, crying for mama, who never looked back but with amazing speed ran up the steep side of the mountain, along with the boy. At her first opportunity, the girl bear got out and ran to catch up.

August 3: I was down at the river panning concentrates. Rich was up in our living room tent, reading, with the windows open. When I finished and went up, he said the boy bear had looked in the window at him, and as quickly as Rich could get out of the chair and grab the gun, the boy bear met him at the door. They scared each other. The bear ran off.

For the rest of the summer, we were not bothered, but we heard stories of three bears being in camps up and down the river. The sad truth seems to be that the mother bear was teaching the cubs to be camp robbers. And once a bear is a camp robber, there is not much hope for a good ending.

July 1993

Our dog had two names: Colt and Doogie Houser. Looks like this summer we were calling him Colt.

We had a bear visitation in camp again. Colt, the dog, and I were home alone. Kurt and Rich had gone to town 13 miles by boat, then 50 miles by truck to Chicken, and weren't due to return until evening.

Colt and I had just taken a tundra hike, checking on the ripeness of the blueberries, which he liked too—he would eat them right off the bush. We were scouting out some good blueberry patches, so when picking time came, we would not waste valuable energy in mediocre places.

He ran ahead of me into the camp. I was still on the outer limits of the camp when I heard thunder—odd, no clouds; or was it sonic boom—no jet streams, either. I did not have to wonder for long.

Over the top of the hill came a bear, running hard, and hot on its trail, also running hard, behind but gaining ground, was Colt! I thought (1) how much that bear looked like a big dog, (2) how Colt's insides were going to look on the outside after the bear got through with him, and (3) shit, oh dear! where is the gun? All of these thoughts happened in a very short time.

I concentrated on getting the gun from the nearest tent before any violence began, while at the same time calling Colt, who was not listening. No sooner did I walk out with the gun than Colt came around the corner of the tent and sat down by my side, breathing hard and barking, without the bear. I was instantly relieved that the dog was back in one piece and that the bear had disappeared.

The bear? Oh yeah. As my focus cleared, I realized I could hear it but could not see it! A ravine fell off beside our tent. I thought the bear was just over the edge. I was afraid to go look because in addition to the usual fear caused by staring a cornered bear in the face was staring one in the face and it taking a swipe in my direction.

So, while standing there with a bear close by that I could not see, I called "Time Out!" I needed to figure out the situation. In that contemplative moment, I felt eyes on me and looked up. Halfway up the first, big-enough spruce tree it had come to and only spitting distance from my sleeping tent, as it was proving, was the bear!

Behind the relief I had felt loomed the big question: What next? When it came down, would the bear leave peacefully or tear down my tent and charge me while I tried to protect the main camp? And should I tie up the dog far enough away from this scene so the bear would come down or just let Colt bark every time we heard a breaking branch and keep the bear up there until the guys or the cows came home? Colt had already given chase and nearly worn himself out messing with that treed bear on an 80-degree day with a sun factor added on. Meanwhile, the bear rested up in the tree.

I eventually decided to take Colt to the main camp where he could get water and rest, secure in the knowledge that when we heard branches cracking, he could run up the hill to the tree and bark a few times to maintain the status quo. It worked great. Even though I was not able to concentrate on much but the bear in the tree all afternoon, Colt got a rest.

I was reminded periodically that the bear was still there by one of three noises it made: (1) crying and moaning, (2) clacking its teeth, and (3) a kind of snuffling the dog makes when he cannot get enough air.

Also, the poor thing was drooling and peeing in the hot sun.

I went around to take a photo of the bear's face, which was only nine feet up, and after eye-to-eye contact, which began to feel as though this was taking way too long, I chose not to stand there and take a photo. That bear could have jumped on me. It weighed many times what I did and had long claws!

I could not stop thinking of the bear in dog terms. Furry and big and brown and not so different looking as one might think, and when it "cried," I was moved. When it sprawled over three big branches on one level of the tree with its snout resting on a slightly higher level, it looked like an Alaskan sled dog, lazing around its doghouse.

This all began at 1 p.m. The guys got home at 8:30 and tied up the dog. Within 10 minutes, we heard branches cracking and when we checked, the bear had gone.

Maybe this bear wouldn't bother other camps now because of today's experience.

The guys wondered whether the experience was a good one or a bad one for Colt. He protected the camp. I appreciated the way it turned out, but did he learn about fear of the awesome ferocity of the bear? Probably not. Or did he think the bear was a playmate?

126

The next time I went to the outhouse, I found pieces of the outhouse itself and poop taken out of the deep hole. I guess Colt heard the commotion and went to investigate when we were coming back into camp from our walk. I hate to think how the encounter might have occurred if the bear had wandered in with no dog in camp. Most years we did not have a dog.

September 1993

At 4:30 a.m., I awoke suddenly, with the hair on the back of my neck standing up. The dog, Colt, was sleeping outside my tent. If any noise had been made, he would've been barking. We were alone in camp in the dark.

As I listened to the quiet, trying to pick up on any noises, especially the unusual ones, whatever had awakened me, happened again. It was a deep, guttural sound, a quarter of a mile away, the sound of one large critter communicating with another one. Still, the dog was asleep, and he could hear better than I, so maybe my mind was playing sleepy tricks on me. After a while, with no more noises coming through the night air, I decided to try to go back to sleep but not before I got dressed in my warmest clothes and located the gun!

About the time I jumped back in bed, Colt started a few little groans of the type he made when he was dreaming. He quit soon and peace settled in. For one minute! That's about how long it was before the noise, quieter and shorter than the other ones, happened again. This time the dog was on his feet, sniffing in the direction of the noise, more or less at attention, and making constant moans.

By this time, it was 5:00. The sky was beginning to get light. At least we would see what we were up against.

I moved outside, sat down with my back to the tent wall, feeling like a sentry waiting for the enemy, an enemy known to be out there but its nature and number, unknown.

Colt was not helping matters any. His quivering nose was pointed in this direction, then that direction. His intensity reached such a level he was moaning all of the time now and a bundle of alertness. I was having a hard enough time keeping calm with my knees knocking together from fear and cold (48°F), without having to witness his uneasiness.

Of all the large animals around here, only three commonly come into contact with human camps. One is the moose. No need to worry there, as long as we did not get between mama and her calves.

The second is the caribou, which like the moose, will walk all around and through a camp to get where they are going. They are people-shy, though, and tend to avoid being seen, a pretty tricky move since they are so large.

I've been surprised to go down to the riverbank within a stone's throw of our camp and find fresh tracks of two or three caribou or moose, tracks made while I was around, but I had not heard the animals passing by.

The third large animal and the only one to ruin my Alaskan wilderness experience is, of course, the bear. One bear is cause for concern, but we had at least two to worry about right now—unless we had one talking loudly to itself! Nothing like bear thoughts at 5:00 a.m., with something moving toward us!

By this time, Colt was looking downriver, the original location, and behind the tent, toward the tundra, the route animals took when we were on the river bar. Walking on the river bar is easier than tundra walking, but the best walking of all usually occurs on the animal trails near which we dredgers tend to put up our camps!

Not knowing where the animal was located created an unease in me, ramping up concern. On the other hand having a gun lent a sense of security, leveling out the playing field, even though I had only shot this gun once before, thirteen years ago at a target. We had other guns I was proficient with, but they were not in this camp. I knew I could do it when/if I had to. I had carried the other rifles and shotguns around for years. All of this does not mean I thought I was invincible. It was, after all, a bear we are talking about!

The tension continued until 6 a.m., when I felt the animal must have moved on down the gravel bar out of our vicinity. Colt continued to growl and sniff, but I detected a slightly lower tension level. We went down the river to check for tracks. Moose.

Late September 1993

Rich and I had begun packing up for the season. We had taken a load to the cabin in Chicken and were dawdling about going back to the camp on the Mainstem. After four days, the BLM rangers came and asked us how long it had been since we had been down to our camp. When we asked why, they told us that a bear had torn through one wall of our screen tent kitchen and had gone out another wall, apparently for entertainment because there was nothing in it, except maybe some smells. We had left a 2' X 4', three quarter inch plywood food box outside, with a one-burner stove, a pan, and a package of rice in it. This was so we would have something to eat when we came back to finish breaking camp. The box had two hasps, locked with padlocks under normal circumstances. However, Rich had taken one hasp off for use with something else. When it came time for him to lock the box to keep bears out, only one end locked.

The bear had nothing but time. It turned the unlocked end of the strong plywood box into toothpicks and took out the package of rice, tearing it open in the process and scattering it into the sand. So, I had another cleanup, complete with shoveling. I must admit, after this summer's bear dealings, I was pretty much done with bears.

August 1995

For five days, I had been hovercrafting around the 40 Mile River system with Wes and Randy DeVore. The first night we had camped on a sand bar on the North Fork in the trail the animals use. I wanted to make camp off the trail but was outvoted even though moose and caribou tracks were all over the place. The site on the trail was level and cleared of brush, which made it easier to use. This appealed to Wes and Randy.

We got into bed in a green dome tent with no windows, which gave the effect of being inside a pea pod cut off from all visual advance identification of approaching critters while still being able to hear them coming. I began to get nervous and tell stories of bears I had encountered in the past. I succeeded in scaring everyone, including myself. No one slept much.

The next two nights and days, we were jittery, even during the days, as we hiked around or dredged upriver from the original little campsite. When we decided to leave the North Fork, we stopped at our first camp where I had told my stories, to pick up the gas we had offloaded to lighten the weight.

In the sand where our camp had been were huge bear tracks. They were the size of a man's size 10 boot with claw marks coming out from that. All of this would have been enough, but the prints were also five inches deep! Randy's 160 pounds, jumping up and down, did not even leave a print one inch deep, and he was holding the two gas tanks, which weighed another 100 pounds! Someone later told us the bear would have to weigh 1,200 to 1,500 pounds to push down so deeply into the same sand.

We still had another night to spend on the Mainstem. I suggested a cabin I had stayed in two years before at Long Bar. When we checked it out, the three windows and door were broken out and down, leaving us more nervous than ever. We pitched the tent and did not sleep. Later we heard that the destruction to Long Bar cabin was attributed to a bear.

27. OUR NEXT PHASE

As the years went by, Rich, Kurt and I were on the prospecting dredge. Given the nature of prospecting, we were not always in the pay. Whenever we found good gold, the production dredge with two or three divers was moved to that spot, where no time was wasted searching for gold. This was an efficient way to run the operation, but I could not get Rich to share with Kurt some of the massive gold production that resulted on the other dredge from our prospecting. Kurt was not with us every year, though, and we often made pretty good gold when he was with us, so the situation was not totally bleak for him. Rich knew the inequity of the situation and tried to produce as much as possible out of the prospecting, which by its very nature is hit and miss. No one else wanted to work on the prospecting dredge.

In our best season, when the whole team dredged up 660 ozt, both the prospecting and production dredges worked the same spot, side by side. For once, all the divers got the high feeling of seeing gold all over the bottom of the river, a rare sight indeed.

Under most circumstances, the fine gold was not visible in the overburden, the gravel on top of the bedrock (the mostly solid rock foundation at the bottom of the river). This time, though, as the suction pulled the gravel away, the gold was all through the gravel and laid out on the bedrock. Kurt said it was the most gold he had ever seen underwater.

Over the years, we worked the three main parts of the river. There were highlights from every one of them.

Mostly, though, it was the South Fork which rewarded our hard work. More often than on the other forks, there was gold wherever we put the dredges. One reason for this was that the old-timers had not mined there too intensively, so the ground was mostly virgin.

We got used to achieving 1 ozt per hour, our goal every time we worked any spot. We always had 100 ozt seasons, with occasional standouts, such as a 540 ozt season, the 660 ozt season, and one spot where we got 3 ozt per hour—27 ozt that day—the best concentration in one spot ever for us! The sluice box had to be cleaned several times during the day when the ground was that rich.

When we sold claims after working them for many years, the people who bought them from us usually made more off of them than we had. We would think spots were worked out, sell the claims, and someone with a different approach would make more off of the claim. Sometimes, we sold claims because they yielded less than 1 ozt per hour. The new claim owners would make plenty without such lofty aspirations. Or maybe, the coveted 1 ozt per hour was located in rapids that we did not want to work. No matter. We produced over 5,600 ounces of gold through the years.

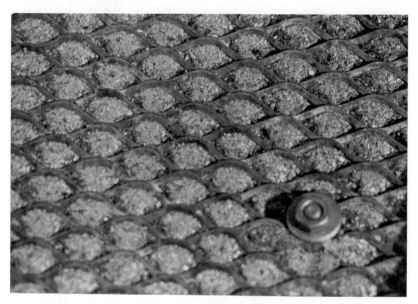

This closeup of a cleanup box shows what a good cleanup of fines looks like! Yes, that is all gold.

One of our team, Joe Taylor, used the gold he earned to help start up a highly successful jewelry store in Fairbanks, Taylor's Gold-n-Stones. His partner was his brother and former 40 Mile dredger, Glenn Taylor.

We worked hard in the summers and lived whatever lives we chose in the winters, traveling and always having what we wanted. The down time was great after the hard work of the summer. Generally, we lived in Fairbanks or Anchorage with three month vacations down in the Lower 48 where the winters were not as severe.

There was paperwork called Affidavits of Annual Labor and fees called Rents and Royalties for maintaining our rights to the minerals in the bottom of the river on every claim. Forms had to be filed and paid for by midnight November 30, every year in the Fairbanks Mining District and could be done in the comforts of town. We also applied for camping and dredging permits during the winter for use in the coming May when we went back to the river to do it again.

On the North Fork, another area of virgin ground, we found several large pockets of gold. However, due to the incline of the fork itself, where the flood water rose and fell faster than on the South Fork, there were fewer areas of gold concentration. The river bottom anywhere acts as a giant sluice box, catching gold in protected areas with its natural riffle system. One summer, Rich and I prospected six miles of this fork, finding no area we wanted to spend much time in. That was rarely the case on the South Fork.

Two things slowed our gold production on the Mainstem, the third portion of the river open for mining.

One: Below the 40 Mile bridge, the river was heavily worked by the old-timers all year round. Finding unworked spots was difficult. To find them, we had to go through many areas that had been ice drifted. In these areas we found burned wood on the river bottom, indicating that someone had melted the ice down through the gravel during the winters.

The miners of olden times had worked up from the mouth of the river in Canada, without many making it too far past Steele Creek on the Alaskan part of the river. This left most of the American portion of the 40 Mile unprospected and unmined.

Two: My body was wearing out by the time we got down that far. We had been mining for close to 15 years by then, and all of our bodies were wearing out to various extents by the effects of repetitive lifting and moving things, such as:

- barrels of gas (50 gallons of gas X 6.25 pounds {at 72°F} per gallon = 312.5 pounds each + the weight of the barrel adds 40 more pounds = 352.5 pounds each),
- the dredges and their component parts, such as the Volkswagen engine for the 10″ or two 16 HP Briggs and Strattons for the 8″, sluice box, jet, pontoons, hose and nozzle, and five gallons of gas every hour,

- the attendant mining accessories, like cases of oil, gold pans and shovels, the gold wheel, 12-volt batteries to run dredges, boats, and the wheel, the generator, and hundreds of tools,
- wood, both plywood and firewood, and the wood stove,
- boat motors, boats, and boat gas,
- 5-gallon buckets of concentrates (gold weighs 19 times the weight of water, so the more gold in the bucket, the heavier and better it is!!) or water (at 8.34 pounds per gallon, a 5-gallon bucket of water weighs 41.7 pounds). I carried thousands of these,
- all sorts of camping gear, clothing, and food for several months,
- up to 100 pounds of weights worn for three hours every day by the divers, their moving by hand every rock underwater bigger than seven or nine inches (depending on which dredge we were using), the tender moving many rocks by hand in the river behind the dredge,
- tugging their diving gear on and off,
- and so many other heavy things.

There came a time when my body did not completely heal over the winter. Even when it seemed healed, the first repeating of the activities in the spring quickly brought back the aches and pains of the last mining season. We all loved being out in nature, doing the mining thing, but there is only so much a body will take.

I remember walking down to the boat, moving camp from the Mainstem toward the end of my dredging career, carrying two arms full of whatever and having my knees just give up, although my knees were not even a known injury.

My biggest problem was something akin to tennis elbow. I tended to carry as much as I could and just a little bit more, so I would not have to make so many trips.

I went back to mining ten years after I quit. Within the first couple of days, my elbows and forearm muscles went out again, remembering after all that time.

We gave our youth to the South Fork, which the old-timers had not decimated. The gold was everywhere, and we still had the physical ability to go get it.

Our time was our own. We set our working hours, or even, whether we wanted to work. We loved the river, the gold, and nature. We enjoyed being our own bosses. We loved the solitude.

28. TRANSITION 40 MILE TO TOK 1996

The simplicity of Tok, teetering on the brink of civilization, isolated beyond most people's understanding, is best explained using examples. For nine months every year, two restaurants are open, as are two bars. We have a grocery store, a small clinic, a post office, and three motels. It is 95 miles to the nearest town more or less just like Tok, and 200 miles to the nearest box store and fast-food restaurant in Fairbanks. Larger facilities are 325 miles away in Anchorage.

Scattered throughout all of these miles and miles of open wilderness are Alaska Native villages in the general Tok area. They don't have a "big" grocery store like 3 Bears in Tok. Their residents shop in Tok or go to the same places Tok residents do for more than Tok has to offer. The names of these villages are Tanacross, Tetlin, Mentasta, Dot Lake and Northway.

In 1996, Rich and I opened Alaska Gold Shop in Tok, AK, the nearest town to Chicken and the 40 Mile with electricity, phone, and running water. Tok is on the Alaska Highway, the only road coming in and out of Alaska, so everyone entering and leaving Alaska in a vehicle goes by in front of me. I have seen almost every conceivable type of motorhome, and yet, every year someone drives by in another manifestation of transporting people on vacation. It never gets boring.

Rich continued mining that summer while I got familiar with running a retail store, something neither of us had ever done. My experience consisted of selling Girl Scout cookies as a kid, which I was very good at. One year I sold more cookies than any other girl in Wichita, Kansas. Rich had done some flea market type stuff. We set this up so we could stay in touch with the gold and gold country as we aged out of mining.

Running a retail store was very different from any work I had ever done. Once again, I was learning something from the ground up. We rented the shop from Chris Marshall, who became one of my dearest friends. Chris ran a welding shop on the same property as my Alaska Gold Shop.

After all those mining years, the 40 Mile lifestyle was second nature to me. Often, the river would call to me, saying, "Come back." Unable to scratch that itch any other way, I would get in my car after I closed the shop at 9 p.m., drive 88 miles to South Fork, get out and stick my foot in the water, stand in the quiet for a while listening to the flowing water and quaking leaves, then get back in the car and drive back to Tok. Many years passed before these urges released me.

The store in Tok, AK, with my 6″ Precision dredge sitting out front.

I had begun years before to withdraw from Rich. As a friend put it, he had a hole in his pocket where most of the money went. The gambling which claimed most of his attention and influenced his attitude toward me had eroded my feelings. Staying was more habit than anything. After he told me he considered everything left of the dredging business to be his and admitted to having gambled away pretty much all moneys, it hit me that we would be starting over in our fifties. I was now motivated to begin the separation process.

If I was going to start over without any changes from his side, I might as well start over on my own. That way, any money that I earned using my abilities would be under my control. And I would not be enabling a person spiraling out of control. Sometimes it is hard to know where the line is between enabling and loving. Somehow, for me that line had been crossed along the way.

Over the years, we had used up my dredge, tents, camping gear and my physical self. Over the next few years, I rounded up another dredge and mining equipment and claims, which you are about to learn I had to earn at great danger to life and limb. And I accepted the store in Tok, which I felt was his apology to me for having made such a mess of our finances, though he did not say so. By this time we were reduced to fractured conversations.

Once, Rich said to me, "Nothing you ever did counted for anything," implying since I was not a diver, actually sucking up the gold, I did not count. Most of the time being a woman dredger is a different experience from being a man dredger. In my case, I was physically smaller, limited in the size of dredge I could handle underwater. Certainly not the 8" or 10."

The gold would not be in the sluice box without a diver, but it is flippant to discount the contributions of the person who works on the top of the dredge or in the cleanup which usually takes as long as dredging it up. We were a team. The divers were happy to let me do the camp and cleanup tasks, as it made their days less strenuous, and my pay did not come from their pockets. I had come into our circle with an 8" dredge, boat, and truck and changed the direction of the team. One dredge found the gold; the other dredge worked the ground. What a luxury!

Here is what I think about not counting for anything: I beg to differ. Since my body gave out long before any of theirs, I might have been working harder than they were... Just saying. Not that I have to justify.

Rich told me in our last intimate conversation as a couple that if he had given me half of the physical gold, we still would have had money. His truth had a dark side: He had not given me half, so we didn't have money. Let's not put a positive spin on the situation. Coulda, woulda, shoulda.

My days of being on the 40 Mile were not quite over. Rich was about to attempt to deviously deprive me of my share of our claims!

On another note, that first summer in the gold shop in Tok was full of lessons, including living in a settlement after 16 years in splendid isolation. Soon after I opened for business, one of the first lessons came in the form of Yukon Charlie, a scruffy looking guy traveling in a school bus. Charlie pulled in next door at the welding shop with some problem

138

that took three days to fix. During that time, he hung around enough that both Chris and I got used to his comings and goings. When he was good to go, we waved goodbye as he headed toward the Canadian border 90 miles away.

The next morning, I looked out the window and saw Charlie walking along the highway with his dog, pushing some metal thing, which he said later had some gold mining function. Turned out, just before he had arrived at the border, the engine of his bus blew up. So, he was back in Tok, only now his standard of living had dropped significantly. Chris told Charlie he could spend the night(s) for free at Chris's house under construction next door while Charlie made his new plan. The cabin had a roof, most of its windows, and a door with a lock. At least it was inside. Charlie was hanging around Tok again.

I had a bus load of 14 tourists milling around my store. I handed them my big 3 ozt nugget, barely putting it back in the display case, not closing the door of the case after they left. Charlie came in and asked to use my phone book. I stepped behind the curtain that separates the shop from the office for two or three seconds. I gave him the phone book. He took it out onto the porch joining Chris and Rich, who happened to be in town from the goldfields. They sat and talked.

During the next few hours, as I went through the day, I became aware that I did not know where the nugget was. Customers came and went, keeping me busy. When I finally stopped all the distractions and concentrated on finding it, the nugget was nowhere to be found.

Playing detective and going over all of the customers since I last saw the nugget, I concluded I should talk to Charlie. I had not seen him since he borrowed my phone book hours earlier. I went out on the porch to locate Charlie, who, as it turned out, had drifted away earlier with neither Rich nor Chris noticing the direction he went off in. We put our heads together and decided to go over to Chris's house where Charlie was staying. When we got there, Charlie's pack, dog, and Charlie were gone!

Chris and Rich told me to go call the troopers, as they jumped in the truck and went looking for Charlie. There are only three roads going into and out of Tok, so Chris and Rich weren't surprised to find Charlie hitchhiking on the edge of town, trying to get a ride to the border. That was his big mistake. Tourists are reluctant to pick up hitchhikers going toward the border because the tourist becomes responsible for the hitchhiker while in Canada. Most people don't want that burden.

There have been several hitchhikers over the years who have spent a week or two in Tok, trying to hitchhike out of Alaska. If Charlie had tried to leave town hitching toward Fairbanks or Anchorage, he probably would have been long gone by the time I sounded the alarm. Travelers are more likely to pick up hitchers staying in state.

Many years ago, someone robbed the Tok grocery store and headed south out of town. When he had gone 60 miles through the middle of nowhere, he came to a bar. He went in and bought a round, thinking he had enough distance between him and getting caught. While he was enjoying his drink, the troopers showed up and took him away. There is no place to hide out there. Most of the time.

Chris and Rich pulled up to Charlie and jumped out of the truck, Rambo-style. Chris, in Charlie's face, said: "Give it back, Charlie. We know you've got it. We have you on videotape."

Charlie said, "I don't have no nugget."

Rich said, "We did not say anything about a nugget. Janice has called the troopers. If you give it back, there will be no questions asked. So, you have until the trooper shows up to take this deal."

Charlie murmured, "I don't have it. You can search my backpack."

Chris replied, "We are not searching your stuff. We'll wait for the trooper."

Charlie thought a few moments, sweat running down his face, then said, "No questions asked?" and pulled the nugget out of his watch pocket.

Later, the trooper said we were lucky to get the nugget before he got involved because he could not have used our techniques.

During the next 25 years, after showing whatever nugget I take out of the display case, I put it all the way up in the front of the case, then shut and lock the door. So, I did learn from this experience. I also learned about certain people, broken down in Tok, hanging around looking for trouble. And I learned don't turn my back on anything valuable. I don't have to worry about anyone wanting a phone book, either. The world has moved on. More cell phones and fewer land lines changed the landscape when it comes to phone books.

29. 40 MILE WINTER ADVENTURE

On December 15, 1998, I got the distressing news that Rich had not paid the annual rental fees due by midnight November 30. He had dropped the claims! What? Why? He wanted to keep the entire dredge operation—both dredges, all eight boats, all three trucks, etc—but no claims. Huh? No dredger can work without claims. Claims give the claimant rights to the minerals in the bottom of the river for as long as the claimant maintains the fees.

Miners had come into my shop all summer with stories of Rich coming to them and telling them he was trying to think of a way to handle the claims so he would not have to split them with me. What he came up with became clear as time went on.

It would have been easier on everybody for him to have come to me and talked it out, of course, but as a testament to what our partnership had become, that is not what happened.

In the meantime, the thought of our claims being so vulnerable to takeover by another miner worked on me. I called the claims office to find out who had picked them up. It could not be Rich; once dropped, the claims cannot be staked by him or anyone else named as owner on the dropped claim location notice, for one year. It could not be his brother either. He's a successor in interest, as are the other members of his family.

Once the claim location notices are posted on the northeast corner of each claim, the prospector has 90 days to record them in the claims office as required by the mining regulations of the State of Alaska. I was told by the Recorder's Office that no one had filed them so far.

Because I was in Tok, the nearest town to the claims, with my store on the Alaska Highway open that winter, I knew that as of this date, no one besides rare trappers had been up the unmaintained Taylor Highway, which ran north through 67 miles of unpopulated, desolate wilderness to Chicken, with its 11 inhabitants. How did I know? Tok has a network of information. No one in Tok or Chicken had seen him around.

I could not email anyone in Chicken because the internet had not been fully established then.

Anyone at any time could go up there and stake the claims. More and more, I was thinking that should be me.

By now, I had worked myself into a state. What was happening to the claims? Then, why shouldn't I have a winter adventure, take a run up the Taylor Highway through the "out there" terrain, with no one knowing I was on the way on the shortest day of the year, at the coldest time of year on that unmaintained road, and as it turned out, alone?

These risks paled beside my paranoia. I had a dependable 14-year-old car; no matter that the odometer had just passed 100,000 miles. As a mechanic said at some point earlier, "It is just getting broken in; it is good for 300,000 miles!" I had no reason to disagree. It got 30 mpg and started as easily as could be expected in the moderate cold -20°F to -30°F temperatures we were experiencing. However, always before, I could plug in the block heater to keep the oil flowing better and the battery heater to keep the battery strong. Now I wanted to leave all electricity behind. "No problem," said the part of me being eaten alive by the desire to go.

I did not weigh in the fact that my car had 13-inch tires, while the trappers' trucks had at least 15-inch tires. I conceivably would be plowing off at least two inches of snow all the way to Chicken, more if it had snowed or drifted since the last truck drove through. Plowing might be the wrong word. More like I would be dragging the underside of my car through the top of the snow on the highway. Talk about wear and tear, as well as increased gas consumption in a land with no gas station. There was also the possibility of getting stuck!

Other things I did not consider would turn up. I was pretty sure I could handle them. Any uncertainty arose out of the simple fact that I was heading out alone into the back country of the coldest part of ALASKA! A man had frozen to death last year out there in his car, but he was a stranger who did not know this land and had not been prepared with survival gear. I felt 16 years in this country giving me comfort, even though these years were May through October with rare trips out in winter in trucks with other people.

I still owned Bessie Mae, my three-quarter ton truck, but as luck would have it, a structural problem led to its being in parts and pieces at this moment, with no quick fix in its near future. No one would rent me a truck. No one would go with me. No one wanted any part of this adventure, as much to stay out of the middle of whatever was going on

142

between Rich and me, as to the idiocy of what I was doing. So, it came down to my four-wheel-drive car.

"All right," I thought to myself, "Let's get ready."

I bought chains. The directions read in bold black print, "Make sure these fit before you need them." I had so much else to do, I did not test them, but according to the label, they were the correct ones. It never occurred to me the label could be wrong, or the wrong chains could be in the case. Well, it did but not enough for me to go so far as to check them out. I went on, knowing I had chains in the car but not 100% sure they fit the tires. If a problem arose and I needed these chains, I would deal with it then, ignoring how much more convenient dealing with these matters would be near the store or at home in the garage or driveway, rather than while stuck in a snowbank in the middle of nowhere.

I was on a mission. I got extra gas. Nothing is open in Chicken at that time of year except the post office. While gas was usually left at the cabin near Chicken, I would not want to stake my life on it. I packed the air compressor for tire troubles, battery charger, two snow shovels, my toolbox, and fluids galore (oil, HEET, antifreeze). I was sure I had covered all emergencies. As it would later turn out, I forgot my ax and a bunch of other stuff, which slowed me down and could have been problematic.

I got together food, two down comforters, a roll of toilet paper, arctic clothing, claim forms, maps, flagging and duct tape. I checked to make sure someone would come looking for me in two days if I did not get back to Tok by a prearranged time, since there were no phones up there. I hit the road on a clear, windless, but warmish -15°F day. Ordinarily, clear means cold, but this was not too bad. On the day I went for it, no snow had fallen since the last truck had gone in or out.

I ate one last civilized meal at Fast Eddy's restaurant, then got on the Alaska Highway, heading east at 10:30 a.m. The sunlight was just beginning its long climb to the low peak of the three-and-a-half-hour day, skimming across the horizon. The resulting short daylight, such as it is 100 miles south of the Arctic Circle, on the day before the shortest day of the year, is pretty much indistinguishable from the shortest day, being a mere seventeen seconds longer.

The clouds were an uproarious carnival of colors—red, pink, yellow, gray, and white—against the blue sky, the colors of dawn and

143

dusk, but also colors of the day, as though the shortened time of light had to squeeze the day's total colors in on top of each other. There was, throughout that day, the constant feeling of dawn and dusk.

I settled into the drive. I think it was inevitable, understandable even, that my mind was working overtime. Did I do this and that in Tok? What was ahead? I needn't have worried. Alaska was getting ready to show me her stuff.

The 12 mile drive on the Alaska Highway to the turnoff at Tetlin Junction had lots of bare spots on its paved surface. Mostly, though, the surface was packed snow. At Tetlin Junction, the Taylor Highway comes out of the north and dead ends at the Alaska Highway. The road was plowed a short distance, up to the sign that said:

DOT warning at the beginning of the unplowed Taylor highway.

That sign was so bright against the black and white world it was standing in that I stopped and took a picture as any tourist would have done.

The road got rougher. I was plowing through several inches of snow between the tire tracks at a level left by the higher-riding truck axles. I went on. Though everything seemed to be going great, I did notice I was not going along as fast as I usually did on this road. At this rate, what ordinarily took one and a half hours was going to take two or three. So? With each slow mile behind me, I moved farther into uncharted territory. Although I had been on this highway hundreds of times, it looked different wearing its winter coat of snow. I marveled at everything. Sometimes, only a milepost number placed me in context.

As well as checking out the surroundings, I was periodically fighting the steering wheel, trying to stay in ruts too wide for my car. Other times, I'd encounter an area drifted over, making the ruts hard to find. Still, it was early and clear. I pushed on.

As I came around the curve at MP 11, I began seeing lots of tracks. "Snowmachiners," I thought, "But where did they come from?" There had not been any tracks until now. As I looked closer, I could see that animals had made these tracks. Before I figured it out, I saw them ahead. Caribou!

"Cool," I thought, "The 40 Mile caribou herd."

For the next 22 miles, I saw hundreds of these nomadic, almost mystical wanderers. They crossed the road in large numbers but only a few at a time, a process that ate up lots of time.

Winter vehicle tracks with Mt. Fairplay, the halfway point to Chicken, straight ahead. Perfect conditions trick the mind into feelings of safety.

Once they began crossing, a few would come out of the woods followed by a few more, then a few more. They were obviously not on a time clock! I was now driving as slowly as possible—about 5 mph, to avoid mishaps, stopping and waiting when necessary.

My spirits soared as I drove deeper into the wilderness. By the time I got to the halfway point, which is also the highest point at Mt. Fairplay, only a few straggler caribou remained.

The road started to drop from this high point. A half mile down is a pull-out with two outhouses, a nice view, and a carved wooden Bureau of Land Management sign, telling about the 40 Mile area. Sitting there covered with snow was Kurt's van with a flat tire. But no bro. At least he was not frozen to death in the van, 30 miles from the nearest cabin, which just happened to be ours. With rare vehicles coming by, I wondered how he had gotten to Chicken.

I drove on, keenly aware of the insecure nature of my warm ride. No one in Chicken knew I was on the way. I would have to make it and make it I did! At 12:30 I pulled into our cabin at MP 63. Kurt was there. I told him I was going to the highway maintenance camp at MP 74 to check some claims. Now, I was within range of what little civilization exists in this part of the world. My brother knew where I was going.

As I drove the 11 miles, I realized slowly that he did not have his van. His snowmachine was not running because it was in pieces in the driveway. What help would he be? Still, I felt safe. I was close to Chicken, and someone knew it.

I went on to the first claim post beside the highway at MP 74. I did an hour's worth of tromping around looking for claim posts, breaking trail through a foot of snow, using lots of energy and time.

The idea formed in my head of driving on the frozen river, as it was faster to drive a quarter mile—the length of a river bottom claim—and more accurate using the car's odometer. I tested the ice by driving all over the area. My car had to break trail in snow that sometimes had drifted enough to make the car seem to float.

All that and keeping track of the quarter miles and getting out to post the paperwork in the failing light, made time fly by without my noticing. It was only eight miles back to where I had started at South Fork DOT, but the day was short. As I found and staked the last of the claims upriver from where I had started, the sun went down. The light faded quickly.

I happened to be at the mouth of Lost Chicken Creek, the farthest I had ever been upriver on the South Fork. I decided to try to drive up the long, steep hill, one mile up to the Taylor Highway. The snow was deep, the grade, steep. I tried four times to push through the three and a half feet of drifted snow. I was only able to make it one fifth of the way up. Each time I backed down to get another running start. Twice, as I backed down, I slid close to the edge of a scary drop off. Finally, I faced the truth: I would not get up this hill in my car. If I wanted to walk, I could wade through three and a half feet of drifted snow uphill for a steep mile to the highway. Then I would have to walk three more miles to get to my friend, Ari's house, the nearest to me, in Chicken. I decided to drive on the river.

I had another decision to make. Should I go eight miles back to South Fork, where I started this river driving, the only place I knew I could get off the river and onto the highway? Or should I go just around the corner and see if I could find Chicken? Since I knew I was close to Chicken, and with darkness closing in, I decided to try to find Chicken.

As I drove around the bend in the river, I came upon fresh snowmachine tracks. Good. I'd just follow them until they went home. I knew the driver had to be staying in Chicken; it was just too remote for joyriding with no place to stay. Or I would follow until I knew where I was. Everything was foreign. I had not been here before. The snow blanket and falling darkness did not help the visuals.

I went past the old dredge, a landmark I thought was at the confluence of two forks of the river, but geographically, I did not know how it related to the location of Chicken. My hope rose, though. I had heard of this dredge for 18 years but had not seen it. As it turned out, I did not really know where it was in relation to things I knew. Somewhere in this area, Mosquito Fork and Dennison Fork come together to form South Fork and Chicken Creek comes in somewhere. Another good thing to take on a trip like this, especially if you wind up somewhere you haven't been before, would be a map of the area.

When I came back around by the dredge, I realized I was backtracking in the now dark world, heading away from Chicken but maybe alongside the airport on Mosquito Fork. There I might, at last, recognize something. Though dark, it was still early – 4:30. I was confident I would find Chicken. I decided to follow some snowmachine tracks I saw on the other side of the river.

I left the tracks I was on and began an arcing turn, heading across virgin snow toward the other tracks.

As I went over a small rise, I heard a crash, but the car kept moving. I put the pedal to the metal to be sure it kept moving.

I no sooner registered all of this than crash number two occurred. All forward momentum stopped, leaving the car at an odd angle.

I was hoping this was merely an inconvenience and not some degree of catastrophe, though something sounding like distant alarm bells was trying to get my attention.

In the dark, extreme quiet of a subarctic Alaskan winter night, the stars were already coming out. I got out, flashlight in hand, to get a reading on the situation.

The car had fallen through the ice in an area with a large air pocket. The ice covering these 18 inches of air was one inch thick, covered by the blanket of snow. Surprisingly, there was one inch of water running along the bottom. The rear driver's side tire was hanging in the hole but was not even wet. I could still run the engine. The exhaust seemed to flow freely into the night air, not back into the car. At this point, the temperature was -15°F.

I had not had one incident all day that scared me as I drove along on the river—no overflow, no cracking sounds—and now this. I was not scared yet. That would come later. Well, maybe one or two shivers went up my back, there being only so much a person can ignore. I sat in the car, taking a break, thinking things over. I ate, ran the car and heater, considered the size of the sky overhead with all those stars, the whole time dancing around the question of what to do next.

The snowmachine tracks would have to lead home sooner or later, wouldn't they? Maybe I could find Chicken on foot, maybe even get there in time to see 60 Minutes. My friend Ari had a generator-powered satellite dish with 50 stations. When I got near Chicken, I was hoping to hear a generator or dogs barking or maybe see lights from someone's cabin, though the darkness seemed to swallow the light, even with snow everywhere.

My car headlights did not illuminate much, maybe because of the angle at which they were directed, more or less toward the rest of the universe. I wondered if anyone out there on one of those twinklers could see my lights. No one, not even my brother, really knew where I was on this planet. So, I had to get out of this myself. I must say, I was already having a real winter adventure. I had lived in this area for almost 20 years. How much difference could being wintertime make? Twenty years would see me through; I could do this.

I honked my horn a few times, trying to stir any of the local dogs and audibly establish my location. The sound of the horn lost clarity and volume because of the snow cover, I guess. No dogs responded. I did it again, longer this time. Wake up, dogs. I knew they were there; I could see their footprints in the snowmachine tracks as I explored the vicinity, trying to decide which of the three possible directions to go: 1) Back to Lost Chicken—sure thing, long way and up through deeper snow; 2) Back past the dredge where I had driven around unsuccessfully already; or 3) Where I was trying to go when the car fell through the ice.

While trying to decide, I put water, juice and food, into my daypack and four extra flashlight batteries and toilet paper into my fanny pack.

At the last minute I elected to go the only way I had not gone: choice number three. Walking in the snowmachine track was pretty easy and invigorating. I got into it. In the dark, the banks of the river looked unfamiliar, somewhat ominous, something I had noticed during the daylight too. No leaves on the deciduous trees and probably even the winter light, turned loose demons of the unknown. Had I been here before? Was there any piece of a conversation heard over the years that would help me locate Chicken? I kept walking in the fresh tracks, listening to the cosmic quiet, hoping for a man-made noise.

There were four households around Chicken proper, two nearer to me and two farther up the valley. Maybe I would even hear a snowmachine. I began to sweat from the brisk walking. I wondered how far I had come up this branch of the river.

I had a flash that I was walking up the Dennison Fork, headed back toward Tok, away from Chicken, into one of the most remote, uncivilized areas of the 40 Mile. I filed that thought and kept walking. Up to this point, I had not seen one thing familiar, not a cliff or a tree. I kept following the comforting track, hoping all the while that this snowmachine rider was not going home the long way.

I did not have a watch. Too bad. It might have given me some idea of how far I had walked. I learned earlier today that walking through snow made me think I had walked farther than I actually had.

Walking and thinking ceased, as I realized I had come to the end of the track. The machine turned around here. Uh oh. Surely, if I was on Mosquito Fork, I was getting close to the highway bridge. Maybe I should break trail and walk around the next corner or the one after that. Thoughts of the bridge brought comfort; there was no doubt the concrete signified other humans. I was tempted to go for it because my brother's cabin was just up the hill from the bridge, but shouldn't I have gotten to it already? And what if I was on the Dennison, walking into the wilderness?

With the realization of what a long day it had already been, I gave in to a beginning need to conserve energy. I did not want to try to walk back to Tok via the Dennison! At that time, I was 55 years old. What in the world was I doing out here, stuck and lost, having this wilderness experience? I followed the turnaround tracks, starting back.

Within a short distance, a set of tracks went off this trail in the direction I was pretty sure led to Chicken. On an impulse, I followed it into the woods. If I did not do this, I would have to sleep in my car. On the other hand, if I got lost, I would have to sleep in the woods. Or just maybe, I would find Chicken.

Walking in the woods was a whole other ballgame. In some of the places the snowmachine went through, the trees grew so close together, I did not see how the driver had the courage to go there. Where I was walking, the trail opening was narrow. Roots caused me to stumble. My flashlight dimmed. Snow fell off branches, going down my neck. Animal tracks were everywhere. I enjoyed trying to identify them. I had my pepper spray. I knew bears should be snuggled into their dens, but I had recently read that we walk over their dens more often than we know. Some of the photos of their dens looked a lot like stuff I had been walking over all day. Also, I had to be ready in case a pack of wolves attacked or I ran into a lynx.

I fell in a deep spot and did not feel like getting up. I had energy enough, but why walk when I did not seem to be getting anywhere! But I did get up. My flashlight had gotten so dim, I thought I had better change the batteries, which helped. I felt renewed.

I came to what looked like an area of frozen water. Was this a lake? Was it Mosquito Fork? I followed the machine tracks across and back into the woods. Before long, I was at another frozen water area. I asked the same questions without answers and kept following the tracks, which crossed another set of tracks. There was no familiar landmark.

The trail appeared to be curving right. We—the trail and I were now a team—came to another frozen body of water, which by now had lost their novelty. I went across. I was starting to wear down, losing the edge, the optimism. I described it to myself as getting consciously numb.

I had been walking for a long time by now, one foot in front of the other, seeing nothing familiar anywhere. Sweaty, I drank more water. My brain, strained by operating at full tilt boogie, made note of each tree sentinel crowding the trail. The goal of reaching Chicken was fading.

As I came into a clearing, lit by the rising moon, I saw not Chicken but a sight that looked pretty good—my car! Sitting out in the middle of the river, glowing in the light of the universe, the car looked better than it had when I left it. I ran to it, if you can call stumbling and dragging each bunny boot-clad foot running, for they each weighed four pounds, or by this time, a ton.

The clock in the car showed the time to be 9:00, three hours since I left. I had walked toward Mt. Fairplay and through the woods for three hours. Not only did I miss 60 Minutes. I did not find Chicken. I was happy to accept sleeping in the car. I had slept in the car or my truck many times. What was different now was the temperature. Being on the river was colder than up in the valleys. Tonight, there was not a cloud to hold in the "heat" of the short day which could result in the cold being more intense.

I warmed up the car, took off all my wet layers, which suck the heat out of a body and put on dry ones. I began the long, lonely night under the Northern Lights. The man who had died on the highway had left his car with no survival gear and without knowing where he was going. I realized how lucky I was to have wandered back to my car where I had all that I needed to give me a chance to regroup before trying again in the daylight.

This brings me to another item that really should be in a survival kit: A flashlight bulb. I did not take one. At any time and especially in the dark woods, imagine how that could have played out. I used up almost two sets of batteries. How long does the bulb last?

Even though I was still lost, sort of miserable and demoralized, the car lent major comfort to my plight. I had everything I needed as long as it kept starting and running. My accommodations were actually pretty cushy. I dozed off, thinking Ari and Kurt were going to find me frozen in some contorted position because I was sleeping in the front seat. I had tried sleeping in the back. The tilt was too much. Plus, I had to climb up front to turn the car on every one or two hours to warm up my little Bed and Breakfast at the confluence of the Mosquito and Dennison Forks or wherever I was. I slept with the water bottle inside my bedding. Where did I hear that tomorrow is another day? I was just hoping I made it through the night.

As the night wore on, I woke up again and again. Each time I noticed my vitality level falling. I was not hypothermic. I dreaded the decision I had to make at daylight. Again, which way to go? I wondered if I had the energy to head back into the woods and possibly wander around for hours without reaching my destination. I did not think so but going back to Lost Chicken Creek and slogging up that long incline would take three hours. Of course, it would take me where I wanted to go. Did I have that much strength?

Around 4 a.m., with the temperature down around -25°F, I awoke cold and started the car. As I waited for the warmth to build back up in my body, which took about 30 minutes to an hour, my thoughts were drawn back to the earliest prospectors of these tributaries of the upper Yukon. They were mostly men who slowly filtered north from the California gold country (1846-1876 approximately). They discovered fine gold up the Stewart, Pelly, and Liard Rivers of Canada, as they came over the Chilkoot Pass, two men the first year, 22 men the next, in ever increasing numbers, into the headwaters of the mighty Yukon. The first nuggets in the upper Yukon area were found right here on this 40 Mile River in 1886, on Franklin Creek—way up from the mouth. This was the strike that everybody had been waiting for. The town of Forty Mile became the largest, most important town on the Yukon for almost 10 years. In February 1888, William Ogilvie, Dominion Land Surveyor, and George M. Dawson of the Geological Survey of Canada, both Canadian government officials, surveyed the border between the US and Canada at the 141 Meridian and found that Forty Mile was an American town in Canada.

Over the next few years, gold was discovered 100 miles down the Yukon near where Circle was becoming the supply center, the largest log city in the world, and Forty Mile's reign in importance ended, as the town pretty much emptied in the rush downriver. In late January 1897, word would get to Circle about the Klondike, and it too would go into decline as the center of mining activity.

The gold was discovered on the Klondike River, by George Carmack, Tagish Charlie and Skookum Jim on August 17, 1896. They filed their discovery claims in Forty Mile. The few people who were still in Forty Mile heard the tale, saw the gold, and packed up and moved to what would become Dawson, 52 miles upriver.

All of these men were living in some of the harshest conditions on earth. What I marveled over at 4 a.m. was an understanding that they too had been caught out on this or some other remote river, battling their own extremes. Mine seemed puny by comparison, except I wondered how much more extreme than freezing to death, things could be.

At 6 a.m., I woke up for the day, though darkness would hang on for hours more, blotting out the light for more of this day than any other because this was the Winter Solstice, the shortest day of the year. I loved sitting in my car watching the Northern Lights. Usually, Northern Lights come dancing overhead when it is cold, resulting in lots of short viewings between dashes into and out of my house. Tonight, I only had to look out the window. Besides, I was not going anywhere until I could see. I'd been there, done that, walking around in the dark.

After agonizing all night, I came to the realization that my only real option for getting out of this predicament was to walk around the corner and up Lost Chicken. I took the same things with me I had taken the night before, when I had walked for three hours, and started out. When I got to the mouth of Lost Chicken Creek, the South Fork had become bathed overnight in overflow, a layer of open water on top of the ice. What a difference from yesterday. I found a way to get onto land and started up the hill.

As difficult as driving up the hill had been, walking was harder, except that I was able to wade through the waist high snow my car could not push through the day before. Two or three hours later, after huffing and puffing my way to the top about a mile up from the South Fork, I was on the Taylor Highway! I walked the three miles to Ari's cabin and knocked on the door.

When she looked out at me through the window, she asked, "Who are you?" For one thing, I was covered with frost from breathing for hours in subzero temperatures. For another, she was not expecting any company at this time of year. After I convinced her that I was just a down-on-my-luck prospector, she let me in, fed me, and let me fill her in on my story about yesterday's adventure.

Since she lived out there year-round, she understood exactly what the whole thing meant. She had her own stories to tell. Even with modern conveniences, Bush Alaska is still the land of pioneers. Since I was without wheels, I settled in, at her invitation, for an unhurried visit. There is nothing like new blood in town to liven things up.

She offered use of her snowmachine, which I accepted and at some point, drove up to my brother's, so he wouldn't wonder what had happened to me any more than he already did. After I told him what had occurred in my life since I last saw him, I asked him to help me get my car out of its hole.

We decided to do it on Tuesday, the next day, which was a mail day, the day one is most likely to see the other townsfolk in Chicken.

L to R: Judd and Kurt rescuing my car

Sure enough, Judd Edgerton, the Cat miner from Napoleon Creek, showed up. The three of us went down on two snowmachines to rescue the car. Using Judd's handyman jack, another item I did not have in my car, and his ax, which I also did not have with me, to chop wood, we jacked up the rear end, put the wood into the hole, and I simply drove off.

When I wanted to follow the snowmachines back to Chicken the way we had gone down to the car, the guys would not let me. They made me drive the eight miles back to where I had gotten onto the river in the first place. They rode the same way to make sure I did not decide to get into more trouble.

I spent four days total on that adventure. The camaraderie, with the relaxed winter pace, resulted in some of the most enjoyable moments of my winter. When I see these same people in the summertime, we are all running around, trying to make the most of the productive days of access.

On December 24, I made an uneventful trip back to Tok to salvage what I could of the Christmas season at my store. After stopping at Kurt's van and picking up the spare, which was flat, I took it to Tok for repair.

When I got to the top of the next hill, I met Mike O'Gorman and Jim Bissel driving from Tok. Before I left Tok, they had agreed to come looking for me if I was not back in two days. Although I appreciated their selfless gesture, I was glad I had not needed their rescue. I had already been helped immensely by a bunch of people in Chicken. Since some of the time no one knew where I was, I pretty much had to get out of sticky spots on my own. That Jim and Mike came out there shows their understanding of the perils of what I was doing. I will always be grateful for their reliability.

Second Trip to Chicken in a Week

Christmas came and went. I waited to see if anyone else was going to appear to stake the rest of the claims. As no one did, I began to get the itch to be the one. I still had claims to stake. My brother's van was still sitting up on Fairplay with a flat tire, and I had the spare in Tok. He had no transportation. Worse, his nice van was a sitting duck for vandalism. We miners have all been in the position of needing gas or a battery or even a place to sleep! Winter adds to it. Stores are closed, and most people are gone. When I closed my eyes, I could see that baby blue van sitting up on Mt. Fairplay all alone. It needed to be at the cabin.

155

I carefully watched Alaska Weather, waiting for "warmth" and no wind or snowing. On January 1, conditions seemed right with a sunny day and all the rest of the prerequisite conditions. Once again, I headed to Chicken. Driving speed was much less than when the road was officially open, but driving conditions were easy enough. I dropped off the spare at the van and continued on.

While I traveled along, I decided to get Kurt and go back the 30 miles from the cabin to get his van. He agreed to the plan, grabbed his toolbox, and we took off. The van is two-wheel drive and not too high off the ground. My car had already plowed off the two-inch difference made by the higher vehicles that had gone before. He would follow me. By the time he got on the road with the van, my car would have been over the road three times that day. Each time I went over it, I made a point of widening the ruts.

We got to the van and changed the tire. Before we headed back to the cabin, Kurt insisted we load the rear end with snow for traction. All in all, Kurt had an easy drive back to the cabin. Dark was everywhere when we got back.

I drove down to Ari's and spent the night. By the next morning, light snow was falling, creating a gray day. But Kurt and I kept to our plan to snowmachine on the river a little. I went to get him. We rode the same machine.

We went down a different way than we had gone earlier to rescue my car. This time we went off the end of the landing strip. I was having déjà vu, and before we had gone too far down that little road, I saw my footprints, making the wrong turn away from Chicken, towards my rendezvous with winter camping on the river. Amazing how that choice of direction set loose events leading to such discomfort.

Kurt and I went on down to South Fork bridge and checked every claim I had staked along the way. Some of the claims had to have flagging tape. The week before, the tape was too brittle in the cold and kept breaking. We drove around, going two miles down to Judd's trucks. We discussed whether to run seven miles down to Napoleon Creek where Judd and his family lived, to see what they were up to. Out here, seven miles is considered close. I was cold, and we had to go 13 miles to get home. I voted for Chicken. We were both hypothermic when we got back to dark Chicken. The wind had been picking up all day. That little bit of snow had kept falling. The temperature was around -35°F.

156

Kurt dropped me at Ari's in Chicken where my car was and took her snowmachine home to his cabin. She took me in, warmed me up, and fed me. I tried in vain to suppress the slight dread rising in me concerning the road conditions back to Tok. Who knew how much snow had fallen along the Taylor.

At 6:45, I took my leave and drove to Kurt's cabin. Road conditions along that stretch of highway from Ari's, in the middle of Chicken, to Kurt's, three and a half miles toward Tok, were noticeably sloppier than this morning. Loose snow was piling up. I was trying to delay the leaving decision, but I think I had already made it. Kurt and Judd had previously told me driving in whiteout is much easier at night; the difference is unimaginable. At night, there is a lot of contrast; in the daylight, the land looks smooth.

Forget claims staking. My mind's eye looked straight into being stranded in Chicken for months, maybe the rest of the winter. While being stranded was not a totally terrible idea, I also had lives in Tok and Anchorage. Nice to be here, but I gotta go.

Taking Kurt's flat tire and his other new unmounted tire with me, I drove out of the Chicken area at 7:30 p.m. into the increasingly heavy storm. This was the fourth time I had driven the Taylor in twelve days—actually, the fifth if yesterday's trip with Kurt halfway and back was counted. The other four were alone. My stomach was beginning to revolt; my nerves had been overworked; my sane self begged to be magically transported to Tok. The Taylor in winter is something else. My adventuresome spirit suffered a moderate attack of cowardice, or was it somehow connected to the reality of the situation? I could hear my inner being saying "Never again will I drive this highway in winter alone; the thrill is gone."

My thoughts kept being interrupted by (1) drifting snow that hid parts of the road, causing the car to be pulled strongly into the snow, hydroplaning, and (2) the straining to see through the headlight-lit snow falling thickly between me and the road. The going was slow. I was taking it one wheel revolution at a time.

At 8:30, 60 minutes and 22 miles after I had left Kurt's, I crossed Logging Cabin Creek at MP 41 and started up the 10-mile incline to Mt. Fairplay, the part of the highway most likely to cause trouble. Occasionally, the drifts were daunting, but for the most part, their bark was worse than their bite. I almost rejoiced with the realization I could

157

be back to Tok by 11 p.m. Talk about counting those chickens again! No sooner did I relax with that thought than I went around a curve, and the road disappeared. All I could see, through the thickly falling snowflakes, was a smooth white surface stretching out beyond with no sign of where the road ended or started. The whole world was smooth and white.

Until now, the darkness had provided contrast with whiteness because the road surface had been rough, casting shading, providing definition to the road. I knew the road dropped off sharply and deeply on both sides, but I could not see where all that happened. What's more, I had been over this road a total of three times yesterday on a packed trail. What a difference a day made. The wind gusted and exposed a small ridge in the road that I used as a guide to move forward. I was on the way again, only more uptight than before.

From this point, matters got worse. The snow became deeper, fell faster, blew around more. Finally, at MP 36, I got stuck up to the doors in snow with an icy crust under the powder. No amount of backing up or pulling forward made any difference. I was not worried. I knew I could get out of this. I had two snow shovels. I got out, picked a shovel and started clearing a driveway to the area of the snow I had ascertained to be the road by walking around, feeling with my feet for the packed surface under the snow.

Ten minutes later, using my tire tracks as a guide, I had quite a nice trail out the back. I was jazzed. I jumped in and backed up with too much speed. Rocketing backwards, I went off the road with the two back tires hanging over the edge of the other side of the road before I knew what happened. Oh me. Stuck again. When I tried to drive forward, the front tires moved in the right direction, and the back tires, probably due to all the snow in the way, could not get back on the road and were dragged along the edge. I shoveled again. I dug everything out four times. Every time the car plowed far enough along to build up a snow berm, its forward momentum halted.

The thought was forming slowly, I say slowly because by now I had been stuck over an hour, that I had chains in the car. Therefore, while the car was still able to move, maybe I should get them and the instructions out and see what could be done. I was sweating; the wind and snow were blowing. I put my flashlight in my mouth and laid the chains flat on the road as far under both rear tires as I could, after digging the car out once more. The car drove right out and onto the road—all tires back on the road. With the instructions in one hand and the flashlight in my mouth, I put the chains on with one hand, while kneeling in the snow. Wonder of wonders! The chains did fit. I would not recommend anyone else to drive out of town in winter without trying their chains on for size. A $16 item, chains that don't fit are more trouble when less trouble is called for. In other words, do as I say, not as I do!

I started driving again at 11 p.m., fighting the deep, drifting snow, and wondering whether I had the strength to get back to Tok. Up around the next corner, the road was blown clear, the snowing almost stopped. The sky was full of stars, and I was halfway home. Just that easily, I went from struggling for survival to easy living.

I had entertained thoughts of turning back to Chicken while driving through the whiteout and had other thoughts of the mail plane flying over in a couple of days and seeing my frozen remains. While gripping the steering wheel for dear life, I had allowed my mind to think thoughts of death and dying after two trips up the Taylor Highway alone in the winter.

At MP 29, just seven miles from where I thought I was going to freeze to death in a sea of blowing snow, the surface of the road from side to side was pounded flat. A whole herd of snowmachines had been up that day from Tok. Driving the remaining 29 miles was a breeze. I did not take the chains off until I got to the Alaska Highway. I got home at 1:15 a.m., totally respectful of the Taylor Highway in winter and totally determined never to drive it alone in winter again.

Relieved to be out of there and tired of frontier winter living, I closed my store in mid-January and went to Anchorage. All relief was short lived as I realized I had not completed what I had set out to do: stake the other 26 claims. Calls began to come in from other miners concerning Rich's having dropped the claims, wondering if they should go up and stake them.

I reluctantly realized I had to go back to Chicken and stay until the claims were staked. I could not keep running back and forth. I had been warned to wait until the last week in March when the highway was plowed open before coming back. I knew I would have an ulcer if I waited that long. I had to go back to Chicken. This time I would take the mail plane on Tuesday or Friday (by this time, the mail was being flown in twice a week instead of once a week delivery all those years ago when I had first gone out there). I would use Ari's snowmachine to get around. No more car-on-the-Taylor adventures. A whole new kind of fun was getting ready to begin. I was hoping that the third time was a charm.

No More Driving. I'll Try Flying.

Determination is a funny thing. Persevere, and sooner or later, everything falls into place. My mind was certain that things were going to work, relaxed as I was since I was not driving to Chicken. I should have been tipped off it would be business as usual. Fog on the departure day kept the mail plane on the ground in Tok at 40 Mile Air from the original 10:30 a.m. departure time until 2:30 p.m. This departure time was the absolute latest time the pilot could go out and get back in daylight.

Tok airport doesn't have a control tower, resulting in some pretty basic flying. The pilots have radios and can talk to the airport. The radios don't reach places like Chicken until the plane is close.

Sometimes the plane gets almost all the way, and fog is socking in the Chicken airstrip. The pilot turns around and takes the mail back to Tok.

When the plane cannot leave Tok or has to turn back, a Caribou Clatter is sent over the radio waves by 40 Mile Air telling everyone in Chicken the reason the mail is not being delivered, for example 70 mph wind gusts in Tok. Then someone at 40 Mile Air will tell us when the plane will attempt redelivery, usually but not always the next day. Residents in the 40 Mile area have to listen to the Clatters, messages broadcast from a Glenallen radio station four times a day for people without two-way communication. In an area without phones, this service is important.

One Clatter had already been sent at noon, saying we would try until 2:30 to leave. I hoped this would not be a two-Clatter day. On the other hand, I did not want to crash into a fog-shrouded mountain either. We waited on nature. Several times that day the fog lifted just enough to get us moving and just as many times, the fog dropped back in. When the pilot, who had flown in the Bush for 20 years got the feeling it was a go, we went for it.

160

Baggage claim and outgoing baggage at 40 Mile Air in Tok, AK. These two shelves serve flights to Northway, Chisana, Chicken, Eagle, Boundary and Fairbanks—with leftover space on top for cleaning supplies!

I was not hanging around the airport all day. I got packed and to the ticket counter by 10 a.m. Due to the fog, they sent me home to await a phone call that could come at any time until 2:30. As a matter of fact, the call came at 2:05; I was back at the counter by 2:15. Vanessa Thompson, the efficient agent, weighed my pack; I was allowed 30 pounds. I had a box of fresh vegetables too, which was going into a sleeping bag in the plane. It got weighed. I even got weighed; I wondered if my pockets full of flashlight, apples, Leatherman, and gloves, along with the bunny boots I was wearing would overload the plane. Cargo over 30 pounds is 20 cents per pound; my overage only cost $4.40, weighing in at 52 pounds. My body, which usually weighs 115 pounds, weighed in at 161 pounds! Of course, the temp was -35°F, so I was wearing lots of food and clothes. I had avocados, bananas, and

tomatoes in my fanny pack and pockets to keep them from freezing. These items brought from Anchorage have high barter or gift value, or I could eat them.

When all of this weighing was completed, my ticket was shoved into my hand. I was hustled out the door to the plane, which was out of the hangar and had a sleeping bag over its nose. It was already warmed up. I got in while my belongings were loaded. Someone put the sleeping bag inside the cabin and stowed my vegetable box inside it. The pilot got in, gave the safety talk, started the plane, checked all kinds of plane stuff, and we were taxiing down the runway at 2:30. These experienced people know how to move swiftly! I did whatever they said to do. I was in over my head, but I knew I could trust them. They've been carrying the mail to Chicken for a long time.

Today this courageous Bush pilot was carrying in the mail at -35°F to people so isolated they rarely have any touch with civilization at this time of the year other than the mail. I felt proud to be part of it, even though I was more like a piece of mail than any real helper.

I was on the mail plane, and that is what counted.

40 Mile Air doesn't fly if the temperature is below -50°F. If they wait around, as they did with the fog today, the temperature usually rises enough. They don't fly for other reasons, such as wind speeds. Surprisingly, they hardly miss a mail day, although they would miss two while I was in Chicken this time.

As the plane flew over the land I have driven through so many times, I could see for the first time, the layout of the land. Maps tell the story differently. I was blown away that one major fork of the river, the Dennison, actually begins only 17 miles from Tok. We flew over this stream, which would lead us to CKX, as Chicken airport is known in flying parlance, flying below the fog. I knew Mt. Fairplay was to the right, but I could not see any sign of it. This 30-minute flight was exciting; I looked down, sometimes seeing the road as it cut a white ribbon through the highlands. When I was stuck at MP 36 two or three weeks earlier, I had the thought that the pilot would see me. Not only was the fog covering the area of MP 36, but we did not fly anywhere near it!

When we were five minutes from Chicken, the pilot used the CB to communicate our approach, giving Robin, the postmaster, notice to start her snowmachine, close the post office, then get down to the airport to pick up the mail. We circled the post office, then went to land. What a rush!

When she saw me, Robin chuckled, "I guess you can't stay away from Chicken!"

When the unloading of mail and freight was done, I was surprised at how large the pile on the snow was. Mail is important out here.

Robin and I waved goodbye to the pilot and loaded stuff on the big, old dog sled she pulled behind her snowmachine. When half of the pile was loaded on the sled, she said she would come back for the rest and told me to get on the runners of the sled.

Suddenly, I was having an Iditarod-like experience, zooming along at 20 mph. I felt culture shock. Thirty minutes ago, I was in town, dealing with traffic in my car. I now felt free. I allowed my body to loosen up, stretched out on soft knees as I rolled with the mail sled, swooshing along on the snow, fine particles of snow flying up. Forget town. I was in Chicken! Wahhoo.

I wished I had another hand; I would have fine-tuned the survival-weight gear I was wearing to cover all of my body. One or two exposed spots were bearing the brunt of the -68°F wind chill we were creating. I wanted to say wait a minute. I tried letting go of the sled with one hand; I needed two hands to adjust stuff. I wondered whether I should take the chance of letting go with both hands. Would Robin even notice if I fell off? The ruffed hoods we wore made looking back difficult, but maybe dropping 161 pounds going uphill would be noticeable without turning around.

We were halfway to the post office. Body parts get cold astoundingly fast! The airport was only a mile or two from the post office. What was taking us so long to get there? Let's see: 20 mph for two miles equals six minutes. Could this be? Robin looked back for an instant and waved. By the time I reacted enough to signal, she had turned back to driving. I missed my chance.

I tried not to envision what I would look like after frostbite took its toll. We reached the Taylor Highway, turned left and began the steep, mercifully short climb to the post office. I still wanted to jump off and eliminate the wind chill, but I did not want to walk up that hill. I stayed on. What was done was done. Besides, our speed decreased as we went up sharply.

My anticipation of stopping increased. The instant we stopped, I was warmer, even though it was -35°F. I ignored the burning skin and helped unload. Judd was there, waiting for his mail, and Murphy, his wife, was there, too. She rarely came out from Napoleon to the mail. What a treat. We exchanged pleasantries while Robin went back down to the airport to get the rest of the mail.

When the mail was taken care of, we settled in for talking.

I waved an avocado. Everyone who drooled got one.

We discussed vegetables, one at a time. "Wouldn't a carrot be good about now?" "I still have loads; want to trade something?" "Onions, tomatoes, cabbage." "Potatoes, garlic, apples." "I have a big order coming from Sam's Bush mail." "My family members are big cheese and egg eaters. My eggs come from Delta (Junction) by mail."

On an unheated plane, then a half hour snowmachine ride home to Napoleon in a down bag at -35°F, the food doesn't freeze because of the deep understanding of their value by the people who are transporting these items. I suspect that people here would eat them if it did. Well, I should say I probably would.

I removed all head coverings, as, at this point, we were inside the post office. Maybe no lingering damage had been done to the spots on my neck and cheek and up one sleeve. They went through a burning phase while we talked, then felt normal.

The propane lights flickered, as the temperature reached the critical point where liquid turns to gel. The distraction shifted the topic of conversation. Judd wanted to leave this den of women and go to my brother's. He asked what I was going to do, and did I want a ride somewhere? I decided to go to my brother's, too.

We loaded my pack and what was left of the food into Judd's sled. I rode behind him on the snowmachine. I was thrilled because I did not know yet that the wind chill was just as bad sitting behind the driver as it had been on the sled. I took extra care getting all the bare spots covered and climbed on.

There were only two places for the rider to hold: A low steel tube frame, which results in holding on below and behind the rider, yielding an odd balance thing, complete with insecure feeling, or Judd's coat, a wolf parka. I tried both. The parka worked best.

A truck with chains had come through, leaving lumps and bumps in the road. Judd was flying low; we were going 35 mph. We were rocking and rolling. Bucking bronco came to mind. Again, I had various holes in my armor, which, at least, seemed to be different than the spots burned on my trip with Robin. This jaunt was three and a half miles but went by faster than the ride with Robin. The damage felt the same.

Kurt and Judd quickly found the topics of men's conversations out here: "Spark plugs, firewood, chainsaw. " "Rifle, drift mine, gasoline." "2-cycle oil, duct tape, football results from the radio."

It was 4:30. Darkness was falling. Judd had to pick up Murphy at the post office and drive 30 minutes home. I had unloaded my stuff at Kurt's. I put all the winter gear back on and rode to Ari's with Judd. He and I started her snowmachine, and with a promise to her to stop back by the next morning on Kurt's and my way downriver, I returned to the post office.

The time was now 5:00; it was totally dark; the temperature was dropping; and the party was over. I helped the Edgertons load up and leave. I hung around until 7 p.m., keeping Robin late. She called home on a short wave radio, and informed her husband, Dick, and the children that she was late. He replied, "I noticed."

New faces were hard to come by in wintertime Chicken, so when one was around, routines got sidetracked. I liked these people; they were friends. I enjoyed the slower winter pace, allowing for more leisurely, deeper relating. We talked and talked until Dick called back, wanting some attention. We said we would continue the conversation another day.

I took off toward my brother's. Before I went very far, I identified the drafty places in my gear, and contrary to the two other times I was in this situation today, I stopped the machine and fixed them.

Another thing I learned today is that my glasses ice over and fog up anywhere, anytime; I decided not to wear them. They were frozen over, even though I wore ski googles supposedly designed to be worn over glasses. I could not see anything, so I might as well not experience the frustration of frozen glasses. Myopic eyes, while not like 20/20, are not blindness; I could see blurry shapes, maybe not every detail, but I was the only person on the road anyway. Surely, I could tell if a moose appeared before me, a theory I hoped held up.

I had been tossing around in my mind what kinds of scary things were out here—lynx and moose did not seem too scary, and bears were supposed to be hibernating. We already knew any hump of snow could be a bear bed. This thought, like a nightmare, would haunt and taunt me for the next two weeks as I checked out claim posts, climbing over humps of snow under which could be a sleeping bear, who's a grump when being walked upon.

I was beginning to catch onto this extreme living. Taking the time to take care of the details made this place bearable, even fun most of the time. Life seems to get easier and less stressful when the details are attended to, along the lines of making good luck happen by hard work. The elements of surprise add enough excitement and suspense, such as "Is that overflow up ahead?"

I wondered how fast I could go. I gave it gas. I tested the limits, getting up to 35 mph. Snow was flying everywhere. The ruts made by the truck with chains, at times, unexpectedly pulled the snowmachine to the side of the road. The rush, accompanying surviving such out-of-control moments, paled beside the reality of being out of control. I dropped back down to 15 mph. The cold hurt mightily at 15 mph; 35 mph was laser cold. Whose bright idea were snowmachines in the first place?

Then, I was back at my brother's. I decided to take inventory of all the clothing I was wearing. I had on a ski mask, down bonnet, and lynx bonnet. Ski goggles. Smoke-ring scarf. I wore a non-cotton undershirt, sweatshirt, acrylic vest, heavy fleece jacket, XXL fleece anorak, and a down jacket. I had on wool gloves and arctic mittens. On my legs, I had wool long johns, sweatpants, and wool pants. My feet were covered with sock liners, hand knitted boot socks, and bunny boots.

Knowing the food I had carried in my pockets added to the poundage, I no longer wondered why I weighed in at 161 pounds.

A Trip Down to Napoleon

Kurt and I were going downriver tomorrow at first light. I had to get ready. We made plans. I cooked a huge pot of food—complete meal in one pan—rice, chicken, vegetables, and beans. Eating gets harder away from home, resulting in poor nutrition at a time good nutrition is needed. We planned to be in extreme conditions; I wanted our first meals ready to eat. Already at 11 p.m., the temperature was -43°F. While I was cooking and packing, Kurt was servicing the snowmachine.

Judd told us he would loan us a sled when we got as far as Napoleon. But how were we going to transport the gas cans, sleeping bags, chainsaw, and the rest of the necessities the 19 miles down to Napoleon?

Kurt found a four-foot-diameter inner tube, which we pumped up with a foot pump. He found an appropriately-sized piece of plywood, attached it with rope to the top, and voila! We had a terrific sled. Ingenuity is tantamount to survival out here. For this reason, almost nothing is thrown away. At any moment, anything could be the piece that saves the day.

If you have been to Alaska, you have seen houses with "junk" around—old cars, heavy metal, campers, and less readily identifiable heaps and piles. There is a reason for this stuff. If a person has to go 200 miles for the wood or the wood screws or eye bolts needed for some project, the cost becomes astronomical. If it is already out there, it should stay out there.

Another cardinal rule out here is: Never cut a rope. Kurt fiddled around with the rope, looping and winding until it was used in its entirety. Personal satisfaction arises out of this type of thing. The rule is not broken, while creativity has been called upon successfully. People in Chicken who saw this sled, Robin, Ari, and the Edgertons, realized what a stroke of inspiration they were seeing. All day, people told Kurt how clever a thing he had wrought. All day, they smiled at this. Days later, they still mentioned it. Cool is cool, no matter what it is doing.

And then, we were off. At first, we checked the inner tube sled frequently to make sure it was tracking correctly and still pumped up. We were impressed at how well it was hanging in there; we quit checking. Anyway, the hoods we were wearing made checking difficult. The ruff along the edge made us have to lean out further than usual because the bulky outerwear doesn't bend. If we looked around to the left, and the sled went off to the right, the resulting whole-body-turn-around, looking something like a rodeo stunt rider, only got us in the position of watching the sled go zipping across to the other side and out of sight as the snowmachine went around a curve or through a dip, throwing us off balance, grabbing for some support to keep from flying off at 30 mph like a human cannonball.

Kurt talked to me through his parka and over the roar of the snowmachine and wind, while facing forward, "mmgamfhoonsie?" which I interpreted to mean, "How is the inner tube doing?"

"I only saw it for a moment as it whirled through a daze of fur and being off balance," I yelled back, "I did not get a detailed look, but I think the stuff was still on it. I'm not sure about inflation. When I recover from the last look, I'll look again to be sure." These words were blasted back in my face. Kurt did not acknowledge. I did not care.

At South Fork bridge, 12 miles into our trip, we slowed down so we could turn off the Taylor and get onto the river for the rest of the trip. I took the opportunity to check; the inner tube was losing air, not too much, but noticeably.

The temperature here was colder than up at Chicken or the cabin because the river level was colder. We drove the bumpy three miles along the trail beside the river to the point where the trail took to the river.

"Let's stop," I said. "The tire is really low. Let's check it out."

We stopped and pressed on the rubber while eyeballing the level to which the load had sunk. Maybe we kicked it a little.

"I think the cold has lowered the pressure," he mused. "Let's go for it. We've got just seven more miles. Let's try to outrun it."

The idea of having eight bulky items to deal with if we lost the sled lent a new urgency to the mix. We hurried.

When we reached Napoleon, the tire inflation was still hanging in there. The inner tube sled had reached near-legend status in one day. Later in the day, when we wanted to take it back to the cabin, empty and still inflated enough to skip along behind, we realized this is one way invention occurs.

Visitors are uncommon in wintertime 40 Mile living. When company does arrive, a festive air develops. Home school is let out. Conversation is in. New perspectives add zest. Something different has entered the daily routine. In this part of the world, few are turned away from the door. A person's home is turned over to visitors. "Are you hungry?" "Spend the night." At this home, they have a guest book. The distance between homes is such that even strangers can call upon the hospitality of these homes and gain access to their lives. "Come in. Have some food." "Enjoy shelter from the elements."

We trooped in downstairs, into the garage/woodpile/laundry room/wood stove area. I took off many layers. The temperature outside was still hanging around -35°F. The clothes were draped everywhere, so they would dry quickly. Today was a laundry day. Four loaded clotheslines competed for space and heat. I stood by the wood stove, soaking up the warmth. People upstairs were calling down, "What's taking so long?" "Hurry up."

The smell of coffee and bread cooking also beckoned. Upstairs, Judd, Murphy, and their two boys, Derek, 16, and David, 13, were seated around the dining room table in a corner of a great room, two stories high, with windows which let in lots of what light there was on this gray, winter day. I entered this gorgeous room and noticed the large size of the logs used to build this cabin.

"Where did you get these logs?" I wondered aloud.

"Up Napoleon valley," someone said.

Someone else added, "This cabin was built in a month."

"No way," I said, impressed by the timeline.

"Yes, way," explained Murphy. "We dragged them down to this area and invited both of our families to come up from Palmer. For two weeks, the family scraped the bark off while Judd and two guys from Canada built the house."

"No nails were used in the construction," added Judd, "so we can take it apart and move it in the future." I looked around at this substantial building and marveled that there were no nails.

It was then I noticed a pile of squirming fur. Suddenly, the pile exploded. Four-month-old puppies raced in every direction.

Murphy laughed, "I don't know what we would have done this winter for entertainment without the four puppies." I saw what she meant. One was chewing on the leg of another one, who was trying to grab a sock from a third. Murphy walked to the stove in the kitchen. Instantly, the puppies' attention snapped to her. They all ran lickitty split to the kitchen, where they watched her every move. There might be some food in it if they looked hard enough. They plopped on a small throw rug in front of the sink, all four in a pile. After a while they figured out they weren't going to get food this time and went back to their mischief in the living room. We watched them for a long time.

As we talked, a plan evolved. Judd and Kurt would go drag birch firewood down to the house. I would run downriver to check out the first five claims in question. Since I was on a new snowmachine, I had little fear of breaking down and being stranded. Besides, Murphy and I got the guys to agree to come get me if I was not back by dark or 6:00, whichever came first. No getting stranded this time.

I left without taking the food I had prepared and without the pack that contained the survival gear. What kind of trouble could I get into? This time lots of people knew where I was going, and it was nice to travel without a load. I was only going to be gone a few hours. Feeling confident, I left the security of the house in the wilderness. When I got to the river, I turned right, going down where the trail had not been ridden on for six weeks.

The trail was not too bad. Occasional drifted areas provided just enough trailblazing fun. The five miles down to the first claim in question went quickly, as I went under overhanging trees loaded with snow, standing and trying to knock off the snow, and in general, letting loose, getting used to snowmachining on the narrow trail.

When I got to claim number one, I waded up to the post and tried to tie neon pink flagging tape on the post. The vinyl broke; -35°F was too cold for it. I tried three times. Finally, I draped and wound.

At claim number five, while going around a corner on an incline, I slid sideways into deep snow and got stuck. The shovel was in Judd's garage. What was I carrying that could be used instead? After looking a while, the answer came back: Nothing. I used my hands and arms to move large quantities of snow. At times, I wallowed in the deep snow. When I was done, I stood up and dusted myself off. The snow was not wet, having been freeze dried by the extreme cold. It did not stick to me, a characteristic I loved.

Digging out was hard work. I sweated from the aerobic work. A small quiver passed over me. My clothes were just a little bit wet, state of the art survival layers with no cotton, the fiber that loses insulating power when wet, actually sucking the heat out of a person's body.

When I had cleared what I thought was enough of a path, I climbed on, started the machine, and gave it gas. I was out and on my way again with added confidence coming from successfully dealing with this situation. To be honest, it was easier than digging out my car, and I did not even have a shovel.

Freedom was all around me. Everything I was looking at and had seen for the last hour was untouched by man. Basically, no human had been here for over a month and a half, and the trail reflected this. I got stuck several times with no major problems.

One of the posts required a long walk in deep snow. More trouble with the flagging tape wasted time. I made it work, doing the best that I could at the moment. We had already had trouble with duct tape freezing, while trying to attach the jar with the paperwork to the post on the previous staking trip, so I was using baling wire instead. The flagging tape was the most consistent problem. These temperatures were messing with an already difficult task.

I was getting tired and thirsty. I stopped to close the gaps in the gear. The temperature seemed to be dropping. Then again, maybe the sweat-wet clothes were cooling my body.

I started back to Napoleon. The trail was pretty good because I had already defined it on the way down. I had stirred up a lot of snow, sending it flying back onto the trail when I was stuck today, on this trip of five miles so far. I skidded around a corner, realizing as I straightened the snowmachine, there was no response when I released the throttle. I was hurtling along at maximum speed.

I tried rapid workings of the throttle, hoping to break loose the ice I thought was in there somewhere, with no response. I reached over and turned off the key. I came to a stop. My diagnosis was a frozen throttle cable. I followed the cable to the place where it went under the cowling, which had to be raised so the search could continue. The cable disappeared into a black plastic box, closed with two screws with keepers, the likes of which I had never seen. More than a screwdriver was needed for this. I tugged gently on the cable and pressed the throttle a few times.

I was standing on the side away from the key, so I leaned over the seat and turned the key. Instantaneously, the snowmachine took off at maximum throttle and left me standing there. I had the thoughts, "Oh no." "I cannot allow you to go without me." "Turn off the ignition." Although these thoughts seemed to take a long time to think, I was able to lunge to my longest stretch and turn the key. The snowmachine continued 15 feet further after it was turned off before it buried itself in a snowbank.

After looking the situation over, I decided the easiest thing to do was to wait for the guys. I was only five miles downriver from them. I could always walk back if I had to. I did not have a watch, but it was still daylight. There was a slight touch of evening light, though. I hung out, sitting on the snowmachine, secure in the knowledge rescue must be close at hand. Everyone was solicitous when I left. After all, I had already fallen through the ice and gotten stuck on Mt. Fairplay lately. With my record, they had to think I might need backup!

Sitting still, I began to get cold. The dark was beginning its approach; the temperature was dropping from -35°F when I left Murphy's, though to what extreme number we were tumbling remained to be seen. I walked around the area to warm up. My feet weren't cold in my bunny boots, but the rest of my body had undergone some sort of drop in core temperature, which was taking its own sweet time rising to normal, if it was rising.

Actually, by now, darkness reigned. I was using my flashlight to stay in the tracks. My mind had not told me once to walk to Napoleon. Instead, it was insisting the guys were going to show up any moment. I found myself sitting down on the snowmachine again. Now, my feet were getting cold. I got up to walk again. As I did, I heard, in the distance, the unmistakable sound I had been waiting to hear. I walked as I waited for them. I was really not warming up.

At last, here they were, all full of banter and chatter. "It is 6:00. We have been gathering birch and did not want to stop for this, but Murphy made us." "The temperature is -42°F; we will need the birch." I tried to feel guilty, but all I felt was relief.

They found the frozen throttle. As we all looked into the engine area, they pointed out the snow packed in every nook and cranny of the engine compartment.

"How did it get in here," I asked.

Kurt informed me, "See the louvers on the front? Breaking trail stirred up lots of powdery snow, which went in through the louvers."

"That is why we have our louvers duct taped shut," said Judd, indicating use #1,001 for duct tape.

Thirty minutes later, I was back in business, idling with duct-taped louvers. We left with Judd leading, me in the middle, and Kurt behind. I did not know where I was in the dark. I did not care.

I knew I was cold, but it did not matter, a sign of hypothermia. I had a touch of frostbite on two fingertips. I was shocked how quickly the cold took over. Hypothermia had set in, but hypothermia doesn't hurt. Wes had told me once that he was out in coldest Alaskan winter and got hypothermia. He said he thought for a while about taking a nap, which would have likely meant freezing to death, but some glimmer in his mind told him to fight and get moving.

172

Judd, Kurt and I were back to the cabin in no time.

The sight of the light coming out of the three big picture windows of the cabin, up ahead on the left, struck me as being a universal symbol of hospitality and life, a scene right out of miners' experiences for 150 years in this country.

When I got inside, Murphy said, "I had to make them come get you."

"Good thing you did. I was stranded again."

"Are you hungry? I made bread and chicken noodle soup from scratch."

Did I hear angels singing because I was so cold I was hallucinating or because I was lucky enough to have stumbled into heaven on earth?

As all six of us ate, I warmed up. The lively conversation included a lot of laughing at the four puppies lined up outside, front paws on the windowsill nearest the table, begging for something, anything.

I said, "I don't understand all the brouhaha when it comes to snowmachines. They are cold and cranky. They take a person out past the edge of safety, then break down."

"And what does it mean to put louvers on a machine designed to ride through snow?" Kurt asked.

"You got that right," Judd agreed. "They also cost a lot to maintain." He has four snowmachines, so I took his agreement as the final word. "Still, what is the alternative?"

"The alternative is out in your yard," David chimed in. "Your five-dog team."

"They cost $500 a winter to feed," Murphy added.

David, their 13-year-old, used the dogs frequently to check his trap line. I saw their tracks all over today between Napoleon and Walker Creeks on our way in from Chicken.

Each dog had its own house, half full of straw for insulation. A piece of big rebar, pounded deep into the ground in front of the doghouse was used to secure each dog's chain.

By now, it was 9 p.m., and the temperature was -48°F. Kurt decided that we were going back to the cabin tonight, 19 miles at -48°F. I had just warmed up and did not want to move, but since we did not know how cold it was going to get or how long it was going to be that cold, I agreed that I'd rather wait it out at home.

Judd loaned Kurt a snowmachine and a sled, which was quickly loaded with the stuff that had been on the tire sled, which, empty, got tied to the back of the new sled.

"Bye." "Thanks." "Great to see you again."

Kurt left first. I followed him into the January night. Going down the quarter mile along Napoleon Creek to the river, I stayed close enough behind that I could see the tire sled skipping along, looking happy, if I had to put a word to it. My spirits lifted, watching the carefree, dancing tire.

At the river I stopped to close up the gaps in the gear. My two fingertips already hurt. The handwarmer would not warm up for another seven miles. A wind-burned spot on my cheek felt like it had been sliced with a razor blade. I hoped I was not doing any permanent damage to my body out here.

By the time I started up again, Kurt was long gone. I had watched his headlight go out of sight while I was stopped. Now, only my headlight held back the black night. I drove faster than was safe or comfortable, hurrying to close the distance between us, straining to catch a glimpse of his light up ahead. I did not really recognize where I was on a river I had been up and down hundreds, maybe thousands, of times. I knew I would recognize the bridge, though.

Up around the corner, I caught up with Kurt, if you would call his waiting for me "catching up." From then on, our mission was to stick together and get home.

I wondered what the wind chill factor is at -48°F going 20 mph? I did not really want to know; it was idle curiosity at work. At 20 mph, we would not be home for almost an hour. My mind had to pass the time somehow.

Edgertons' house seemed to be in the coldest spot in and around Chicken. By the time we got to the cabin, the temperature had actually risen to -38°F! Overnight, the lowest we saw was -42°F. Later, we learned Napoleon got down to -60°F.

In these temperatures, it would be four hours before the cabin logs and mattresses would be warm again. Rebuilding the spruce coals took time. We carried in the stuff from the sled while we were waiting for the heat to build up. The work helped keep us warm. When the coals were established, we filled the wood stove with birch, the emperor of cold weather wood in our area, on top of the spruce.

One thing I learned over the years is: When reheating the house, throw back the covers or the mattress will be the last thing warm. You cannot get to sleep on a cold bed which is draining the heat out of you.

I got into the bed before it was warm enough, but at midnight, the patience to wait longer was gone. Brrrrrr. I was still wearing most of my clothes, which I would remove only when I got too warm. After a day of hypothermia, warmth was a necessity I could not seem to get enough of. I knew it was only a matter of time, though. The wood stove was cranking.

In the morning, an intense chill hung in the room, as the wood had burned up and the temperature outside dipped down to -42°F. Our forays into that world amounted to jumping out of bed, running outside, grabbing an armload of wood, running back in, loading the stove, then jumping back into bed or filling the coffee pot, then jumping back into bed.

Today, we would jump in and out of our beds a lot. I was reading books Judd and Murphy loaned us, books detailing the fascinating histories of 40 Mile and Dawson City, Yukon Territory, Canada, scene of the Klondike Gold Rush. Dawson is a place related to 40 Mile by proximity and gold. I have heard the 40 Mile, Klondike and the 60 Mile Rivers are in the same goldfield, an expansive area in eastern Alaska and western Yukon.

Time has not changed the scene much around here in the 110 years since gold was discovered on the 40 Mile River. Signs of man's presence are few and far between, especially the farther one gets from the road. Many lives have played out here, lives whose stories rival the adventure stories of mankind since the beginning of time, stories that include my experiences out here which are the dream stuff of many city folks. I am told by my Anchorage High School friends at reunions and by an orthodontist friend in Memphis, among many others, "You have the best of both worlds: Chicken in the summer, Anchorage in winter," the Alaskans say. "You are living our dreams," many of the others say.

That routine of being a snowbird from Chicken is pretty nice. I was doing it in reverse today. I was a snowbird from Anchorage.

We heard on the radio, the weather was cold in Anchorage too. For Anchorage, -30°F was cold indeed. They would go on to set a record for the number of days without going over 0°F. In a way, cold is relative. Chicken and Tok have -20°F and -30°F routinely, so -30°F is not unusual. Anchorage is used to 0°F to -5°F; -30°F there is cold. When the real cold settles in for days, the temperature is almost irrelevant, but every degree does matter.

Some 40 Mile History

The early non-Native residents of the 40 Mile drainage were fur traders, missionaries, and merchants. The hardships imposed on any travel, winter or summer, were complicated by things like no roads, no four wheel drive, no 55 HP Johnson outboards.

If old-timers had boats to help carry their loads, they had to pole or line them through rapids or upriver. The canyon, where the river is turbulent during floods, took many lives and much *gear*. In recent years, people have also died there. Bad rapids are bad rapids, today or yesterday.

In winter, travelers along river highways increasingly used dog teams, making travel somewhat easier, but Mother Nature was just as brutal then as now, and as I was learning, small mistakes can grow out of proportion here.

"The Yukon bason is a region of extremes: of endless summer daylight and sunless winter twilight; of temperatures which peak near one hundred degrees Fahrenheit and plummet to eighty degrees below zero. Here, over a thousand miles above the mouth of the Yukon River, is some of the harshest and most challenging wilderness in the world. It is a land where you strip down in comfort to bare skin in the summer heat, while only a few inches below your feet, the ground is perpetually frozen. The differences between the seasons are equally extreme. There are two major seasons, summer and winter, and compressed between them are two dramatically rapid transition periods. The condition of the Yukon River forewarns of these seasonal transitions, with winter freeze-up in October and spring break-up early in May. The temperature stays below the freezing mark for seven months of the year." Gold at Fortymile Creek, p.4

Reflections on Alaskan Winter

From my viewpoint, the deciduous trees here lose their glorious yellow leaves so fast, I can hardly enjoy what used to be my favorite season. Around the first of September, the leaves are at their peak, lasting roughly one week, after which, for the next eight and a half months, the trees are skeletons, as bleak looking a symbol of winter as exists in this country.

In the spring, the reverse of this phenomenon is true. Toward the end of May, a green glow begins to appear all over the countryside. The buds on the bushes and trees swell and turn green in sync. During one amazing week, most leaves pop out. Summer reigns again, as the world turns green all at once.

Today, this world was white and black. Black spruce, named for its black limbs, with snow covering its green needles, a portrait in black and white, made the landscape scary. At the edge of the clearing around the cabin and into the forest a very short distance, all light was sucked out by the darkness of the trees. Anything could be lurking very close, and I could not see it. We were alone in the cheery cabin in this very remote setting.

The emptiness seemed to grow in size in the fall and winter. Animals were around less often; I did see tracks though. Hares and foxes came and went. Almost all of the birds were gone, but the loyal ravens and the personable "camp robber," as the gray jays were called, stayed.

And most of all, the quiet is separating. No man-made sounds from Chicken intruded on our days. These sounds are a daily occurrence in the summer, when the Cat miners came back and fired up their bulldozers during the day, while firing off the cannon at the bar at night.

The weather conditions were settling in to the meanest yet this winter and would remain tough for the next few weeks, the kind of weather that makes even the arctic animals stay hunkered down. There is a sound that cold makes. This cold was screaming! As I looked around at -45°F, I saw the spruce and birch trees; could the sound be coming from them? How can they live out here? The air had a brittle quality.

The hairs in my nostrils froze at -35°F. I could actually feel the cold spread through my lungs as I breathed it in, undoubtedly not a good thing. The worst was my left eye, which burned a lot. What did I do to it that -42°F day I rode the snowmachine without my goggles? The same temperature frostbit those two fingertips on the snowmachine, whose hand warmers had a hard time keeping up. Every error was magnified. This cold went for the jugular, especially if it was uncovered. All parts of the snowmachine were frozen solid, requiring a propane torch for prewarmed starting. Human life took on a different rhythm. Feed the fire. Get back in the bed that's elevated four feet above the floor for this very reason. Read. Read. Read. And Talk. Talk. Talk. If someone else is around. Going outside, even for a minute, requires elaborate preparations. How could it be so cold? The locals told me about last winter when for two weeks' time, the temperature was never warmer than -50°F, and mostly lower than -60°F.

I wholeheartedly embraced my environment, though. I wanted to know what made Chicken tick in the winter. I was in awe of the few folks who live there all year. Ari, a year-round resident, had been my summertime friend for years and mail correspondent in the winter. Two couples lived here, home schooling their children. And four single guys, spread way out. All called this place home.

My brother was reading science fiction. We could be wherever we wanted to be, by the choice of the books we read. I wanted to read as much of *Gold at Fortymile Creek* as I could. Once I put it down, I did not know if or when I would get back to it. I would have to return it to the Edgertons before I left.

That night at the cabin on the hill in the extreme cold, I felt close to those men and women who came here first.

Why? I would say the self-sufficiency gained out here makes a person feel great, and the prospect of today's down-and-outer turning into tomorrow's top of the heap must have appealed to lots of these prospectors and miners.

My reason was being told I could retire on a sailboat in the Caribbean after one summer. It did not occur to me to wonder why everybody wasn't doing it, which might have been a good question. No matter the reason, I now felt kinship to the miners who came before and after; I too have known extreme isolation by today's standards in America. A four-wheel-drive truck on the unpaved Taylor Highway might look like a chariot to yesteryear's miners, as it speeds along at 55 mph during the summer, but once we were in our mining camps without electricity, phones, and running water, we were closer to the old-timers than to modern American life.

Let's Get This Staking Done!

The temperature outside during the day seemed to maintain; at least it did not get any colder. We decided to wait to go back downriver until there was a break in the weather. That decision made, I started getting antsy to go see what Ari was up to on this cold day, but I would wait until tomorrow to find out.

A couple of years ago, Ari's oil stove quit working when the oil got too thick to flow after three or four -60°F days. Not having an alternate source of heat, like a wood stove, she took to her bed, piling on all the covers in the cabin and many clothes. She did not want to bother anyone. Her fingers got frostbitten. Robin noticed Ari had not been to the post office on a mail day and stopped by after work. When Ari did not answer the door, Robin went in and saved the day. Nowadays, Ari had a backup wood stove and a big pile of wood as another part of life in Chicken.

Ari and I were friends from the day we met in 1989. She was an elegant woman, so cute with her perky ponytail. We talked current events, local gossip, and every other thing we could think of. She asked questions about the things in my life that I value. Not many others knew me as completely as she did. Over the course of our friendship, we watched the O J trial with equal fascination on her satellite TV, run by her generator or the inverter, a solar charger and electricity storage in a bank of batteries, which ran the TV up to 12 hours. We watched ballet, opera, and symphony, as well as great movies, old and new. Football, ice skating, and the Olympics held our interest. We had the ease that comes from similar interests and familiarity. When I showed up at her door, she made room for me to stay as long as I wanted, or sometimes, she ran me off. In the winter with fewer people to choose from and the code of the country, my odds of getting in were great. Besides, she had already invited me this time. I was expected.

After hanging around for a week between Ari's and our cabin, the temperature broke enough for Kurt and me to prepare to go down the river and finish the staking. We loaded up, and with no glitches, made it down to Napoleon, where we checked in, then continued on down 12 more miles.

Before dark, Kurt and I got down to the little plywood A-frame where we were going to be staying. We took our bedding and food inside, then dug out the woodpile. Getting a fire started was high priority, as was assessing the available wood, which seemed to be plenty. We had promised the owners of the cabin that we would resupply the pile before we left. We had Kurt's chainsaw and plenty of time. We carried in many armloads for easy access during the night.

In the fading daylight, we played with the snowmachines, making a circular driveway, checking gas, and repacking our loads for the next couple of days' claim staking. By total dark, we were finished outside.

The shelter was made with three-quarter-inch plywood and no insulation. In milder weather, it was probably comfortable, but with the temperature falling from -30°F downward, the plywood did not hold in much heat. Anticipating this, we had piled snow as thick and high as we could against the outside of the building for whatever insulation it would give us. When we left two days later, hardly any snow had melted though we had a fire roaring the whole time.

We decided that one of us would sacrifice sound sleep keeping wood in the stove all night. Next night, we'd switch. The cold pushed in from all directions against the warmth, attempting to claim back the small patch of heat in the frozen world around the cabin. Burning wood made sleep possible until not enough remained to hold back the overpowering cold. If Kurt woke up cold on my night to feed the fire, he did not have to get out of his bed. I would wake up soon and feed the stove, allowing us two more hours of warm sleeping by extending the circle of warmth once more.

In the morning, we cranked up the stove, waiting until maximum heat output before getting up and making coffee. The temperature outside was -34°F! Shortly after getting up and running, we heard snowmachines in the distance. Judd and David, out on their own adventure, stopped to check on our agenda for the day. The temperature at Napoleon was -44°F.

We all left at the same time. At the confluence, they went up the North Fork; we went down the Mainstem.

We located posts, wading in deep snow to get to them, put up claim location notices, fought the cold to tie the fragile tape, and in general, enjoyed the freedom the snowmachines allowed.

We got back to the A-frame with enough light left to haul in the night's wood and get tomorrow's gas together. There was no sign of Judd and David.

Next day, we finished the staking. Because we had not had any problems on this trip, Kurt went back before I did, leaving me to post the last two claims, halfway to the A-frame from where we were.

Because we had had a full day and I had not had good sleep, my slogging to the posts was pretty slow. I thought to hurry up in case something had happened to Kurt but could not move my feet any faster.

We had unloaded gas three miles down from the A-frame. I paused to pick up the container, which was gone. I saw Kurt's footprints going toward the bend up ahead. A little further up, there he was, pouring the gas into his machine. When he ran out of gas, he walked back to get it, hoping for a ride, instead of walking up to the main camp, where he would for sure have to walk back with gas, if I did not come before he was done walking back and carrying gas.

After getting back, resting up and having a cup of coffee, we went to work on the woodpile. We had used most of the available wood in just two nights! Several hours later, we were done, and not wanting to use any of the resupplied pile, we loaded the snowmachines and headed upriver with an hour or two of daylight left.

By now, the temperature had dropped to -50°F. With night approaching, the temp was still falling and would bottom out at -60°F before our trip was done. At 20 mph on a snowmachine at -60°F, the wind chill was around -95°F.

We wanted to get home before this turned into a tragedy. Frostbite was trying to get a grip anywhere it could. My left eye was stinging; Kurt's fingers were. Several times on the way up, Kurt's throttle linkage froze up, necessitating taking his gloves off at a time no one should have, while touching metal which sucked out what little remaining warmth he had. Serious business.

We stopped at Edgerton's to check on Judd and David, who were home safe and sound, having come back yesterday without us seeing them. We did not even turn off our machines. After brief planning of a future rendezvous, we were off for the trip home with all of the staking completed.

All in all, I was in 40 Mile country for most of six weeks. I saw only the few locals I have talked about, yet it was one of the most memorable periods in my life. In early February, I took my leave on another mail plane, with a heavy heart but knowing it would not be long before the road would be open, and I would be back, under the familiar circumstances of summertime.

30. OH NO

Two years passed since we went through the location process. Now I had to file assessment work on these claims. No problem. I had the required work done, the paperwork ready. As I made my way to the Recorder's Office in Anchorage on the last day, I thought back to how difficult the original location work had been, glad I did not have to do that again!

When I plopped the paperwork onto the counter at the claims office, I was feeling the satisfaction of a job completed. The crushing blow came when the clerk told me the filing could not be done in Anchorage, that it had to be done in Fairbanks by 4 p.m.! The time right then was 1:30 p.m. This could not be happening!

In this age of computer networking, how could it be that the Recorder's Office in the Anchorage District was not able to write a receipt involving no changes to the procedure except the location of the office. Fairbanks District is another recording district in this same state, following the same deadlines and rules, in the same DNR system? Pul-leaze.

I asked whether the paperwork could be faxed. No. She suggested UPS or FedEx, the nearest one a block and a half away. With two and a half hours left before the deadline and UPS so close, I allowed myself to relax a bit. When the UPS clerk told me they had no service that would even be leaving Anchorage, much less getting to Fairbanks Recorder's Office in time, I was back to full uptight status. She was nice enough to call FedEx for me. No. One of them checked with the airlines flying between the two cities. No afternoon flights. They suggested I drive out to the airport and check with Northern Cargo or Alaska Airlines Cargo for solutions.

By now, time was running out, and snow had started falling hard. The drive to the airport was sloppy and slow or so it felt in view of my urgency, confounded by my slowly dawning acceptance that this might not work out, and I might be making another winter trip to 40 Mile. I gave it my all though and went to the cargo places. They sympathetically checked. No go. I had reached a point of resigned submission. I got my humor back momentarily and asked how much it would cost to charter a jet. More than those claims are worth was the answer.

Scenes from the first postings went through my mind. I could not do it again. Period. On the other hand, I could not let just anybody else have the claims. I had no choice but to find someone who wanted them. I called Chris, who had prospected them while on a boat trip down the 40 Mile that fall. He enthusiastically said yes if I would help him locate them. He would meet me in Tok, where he lived.

Chris Marshall, man of many abilities, and his airplane.

I began the task of gearing up for another winter trip on the 40 Mile. This time I knew more how to go about it. I located my extreme cold weather clothing, got together the paperwork, and bought food and gas. While driving the 325 miles to Tok, my mind worked overtime. Did I get everything? I only wanted to do this once more.

I met up with Chris in Tok. The weather conditions were as good as they get in December in Alaska. No new snow was forecast; temps were around 0°F. From the limited information we had about conditions on the river, today seemed to be the time to go, although we weren't certain whether the river was frozen enough for snowmachines. We decided to go for it.

As we drove up the Taylor Highway, we were surprised how good the road was. Along the way, we saw small groups of the 40 Mile caribou herd. By the time we got to Chicken, we had seen 200 caribou and three bull moose. Daylight was beginning to wane.

We borrowed Ari's snowmachine for the trip down to Napoleon where my brother's new snowmachine was stored. Kurt had gone to Hawaii and had given us the go ahead to use his machine. Two machines would give us a safety factor.

The Edgertons helped us fill out the new claim markers supplied by the BLM, a job that took four of us three hours to complete. They were not dredgers, but he was the president of the 40 Mile Mining Association and she the secretary, so they knew something about these new stipulations.

One stipulation was to hang the claim marker on the downriver side of the post with no flagging to announce its presence. Claimants were to use BLM-supplied black plastic, actually waterproof, virtually invisible, screw-apart claim form containers and aluminum sheets to scratch the information onto. These markers were pretty much undetectable to everybody, even the person who put up the posting. These containers were a delight to use, for different reasons than BLM had us using them. They wanted invisible. We wanted waterproof, after the plastic bags and duct tape that we had used in the past, which deteriorated quickly in these extreme conditions or glass jars with tops that rusted on tight. Both were difficult to deal with.

This might have been a great idea for some recreational rafters desiring a pristine wilderness experience with an aversion to anything alluding to the river's rich gold history. It was not such a great idea for people trying to find the posts.

We discussed the thinking behind this latest attempt to deceive recreational floaters into thinking the past and present mining history of this river did not exist. In the meantime, active modern miners would run up and down the river, looking for their own and others' almost hidden claim posts.

Chris and I staked these claims in December, using the new BLM system, which seemed to disregard the State claiming rules, requiring visible posts and paperwork, marked clearly with flagging tape. We were blissfully unaware that at some point that winter or the next spring, the issue was resolved between the State and BLM, resulting in a return to the State rules, so if he would be so kind as to gear up and make another run downriver at much inconvenience and expense to him and just reflag those posts, he could be legal again, by this month's definition.

After spending the night at Napoleon, we got advice about how to break trail and took off. I was in the lead, with Chris following. He was pulling the sled loaded with our gear since we were going to have to spend at least one night in the wilderness cabin at the confluence of the North and South Forks. No one knew its condition.

I had no chance to get accustomed to the rigors of snowmachining. Immediately, as we left Napoleon, turning toward downriver, there was no trail. The ice had heaved up at all angles, leaving me no clue where to go. Two years ago, this same area was smooth as an ice skating rink. I did not have reverse on my machine, so if I got into an ice canyon with no outlet, we were in trouble. Today, though, the river was forgiving. We went the mile down to the corner, slowly but surely. By the time we got that far, I was gaining confidence. Although the ice was a mess for several more miles, we picked up speed.

Soon, we reached a point where we had many miles of smooth ice, where our only concern was open water. The quiet of the snow-covered scenery mellowed out both of us. The sun was shining on the mountain tops; at this time of year, the sun was not high enough in the sky to reach down into the river valley. The day was glorious.

We arrived at the cabin, 15 miles down from Napoleon, and dropped the sled. We kept going, for the day's staking. Around the corner from the cabin was a long straightaway leading to the confluence, the place where the North Fork converges with the South Fork. As we progressed down the South Fork, awareness dawned on me that something was amiss. The closer we got, the stranger things seemed.

Suddenly, we were looking at a scene that could have been on another planet. The river had frozen slowly with unusually high water, causing jagged chunks of ice to push upward 10 feet. We could not even see across the river, making the ice at Napoleon look like child's play. This phenomenon is called pack ice. Using the confidence I had been gaining all day, plus the knowledge that we had come too far to give up, I boldly went into a canyon between two ice cliffs. The snow/ice was smooth down there, but I could not see ahead to where it all led. I turned my thoughts over to the experiences of the day and trusted that we would make it through.

185

Almost as soon as I did, I was faced with the scariest situation we had seen so far. A 10-foot ice cliff stood on the right, open water ran along the left, and the ice bridge we had to go over was three feet wide in between. There was nowhere to turn around, even though the bridge looked too fragile to support the weight of the machine and me. This was the beginning of the trip through all this upheaval. What would we encounter further on if we made it through this spot?

There was no time for thinking. I had to go on. I could neither turn around nor back up. I heard a crack as I went over. As soon as I could, I stopped and looked back, checking whether Chris had made it. He had. For the next two miles, we were caught in this ice canyon, not knowing when or where it would end, with no other tracks to guide us.

When we came out of this interplanetary-looking landscape, the river became smooth and familiar again. We barreled through the peaceful scene, snow flying in such a cloud we could not see each other's machine, only the disturbed snow hanging in the air. The thrill of testing the limits of speed vs. control was offset by the fear of going past the limits. I had experienced the same phenomena the last time I was out here doing the same thing.

We posted claims and played on the machines all day, which was shortened to five hours between daylight and dusk. On our way back in the darkening light, we encountered a shelf that had broken off after we had flown over on our way down. We almost took a bath in the open water, which we could not see clearly. Our luck held. With water lapping on the treads, we drove through, while keeping our feet dry!

Back at the cabin, we realized we were going to need lots of nighttime wood since both the wood stove (at least, there was one!) and the cabin had seen better days. Both had plenty of ventilation. Later, as we looked around, we found that the many holes in the cabin had been stuffed with wads of people's clothing, some of which the squirrels had pulled out and dropped wherever, using the resulting holes for access to this spruce cone storage facility and cafeteria. Several huge piles of eaten and uneaten cones were in our beds.

We went out and took inventory of the woodpile. Chris cut down some nearby dead standing. We dragged it back and made a pretty impressive pile. Or so we thought.

We built a fire, cleaned up the squirrel garbage, made our beds, and settled in for the night. One or the other of us got up frequently, adding more wood to that insatiable stove. The night was long. Our sleep was broken many times. Neither of us got much rest. In the morning, we hurried to eat and get ready to finish the staking.

We wanted maximum use of the short daylight for safety and seeing the posts. We set out, exhilarated by the freedom of being the only humans out here, wading and playing in the snow getting to the posts. Knowledge lurked in the backs of our minds that at any moment circumstances could occur to change things.

With our staking done, we were packing to leave the cabin when David showed up on his machine. He had spent many winters out here. At the ripe old age of 15, he understood winter on the 40 Mile in a way many adults did not. With us on one end of his journey and home on the other, he was confident that he was safe, so he had come down to see us. He guided us home, again in the dark.

At Buckskin Creek, where the water was deep during the summer, David went to the side; we went straight up the middle, me following Chris, into overflow. Chris's rig threw slush up onto my face and windshield, which froze instantly, leaving me and the windshield covered with ice. Duh. Why weren't we over where David was? His experience was far greater than ours out here.

I was not able to see what I was driving into. I was confused by the sudden darkness, which resulted from the frozen windshield blocking out the headlight and my ski goggles being covered with a sheet of ice. Chris kept going, not knowing anything had happened. Both he and David finally realized I had disappeared after they went around the corner, and one of them turned around to see only darkness.

Fortunately, when I stopped in the overflow to clean the windshield and my goggles, I had not made matters worse. The warmth of the snowmachine, if stopped long enough, might cause the ice to melt. Then the tracks can freeze into the liquid as the whole mess refreezes. Stopping can also cause weakening of the ice and breaking through.

However, I was able to continue, with only minimal throwing of overflow back onto myself and the windshield. That said, I was already covered with more than enough ice to interfere with my comfort.

Still, the temperature was warmer than my last outing with Kurt, and we were only eight miles from Napoleon. When David came back, I was out of the water, trying to get up enough speed to catch the guys.

Back at Napoleon, we reorganized the machines after a relatively uneventful finishing of the trip if one doesn't consider the occasional getting stuck in deep piles of snow and being high-centered on a rock, which by now, count as par for the course. All three of us were energized by the thrill of conquering the wilderness. This is an easy feeling to come by when looking out the window of a warm cabin, outlined with colored Christmas lights. Those lights were so lovely in the extreme setting. They lent a measure of man-made beauty to rival the natural beauty all around them. They left an impression in my heart and mind that has lasted for the intervening 20 years.

Judd had spent the day in his workshop, readying his mining equipment to go when the land allowed. Before he came into the house, he called us outside to see the living accommodations of the hens who laid the breakfast eggs. He led us over to a small building with no windows which had a sign saying, "Chicken Condo." When he opened the door, three hens were going about their daily business inside the little room insulated with the thickest layer of batting I have ever seen. The room was heated with an incandescent light! Out here in one of the coldest parts of the world! Those chickens did not even know what was going on just outside their door.

This was when Judd said, "The eggs these girls lay cost $7 apiece!"

"How's that?," Chris asked.

"By the time one considers the cost of generator fuel to run the electricity to power the light, the building itself, and the other costs such as chicken feed, that's the cost."

Talk about putting things into perspective!

Another way to put things into perspective! Edgertons got this nugget in a big cleanup many years ago. This weighed 11.65 ozt; a troy pound of gold is 12 ozt. This is almost a pound of gold!! A one ounce nugget is rarer than a 5 carat diamond; this is almost 12 ounces.

A congenial evening, recapping events of the last two days and anything else that came into our minds and eating Murphy's fabulous cooking, made us forget that the nearest neighbors were 15 desolate miles away. Our heartfelt thanks went out to these people who helped make this potentially dangerous trip safer and so much more bearable.

When we left the next day, Chris spent an hour at the landing, warming up the truck with a propane heater, while I drove Ari's snowmachine back to Chicken, visiting until he caught up with me. On our way back to Tok, in the area where we had seen two of the bull moose on our way in, we found an antler in the middle of the road.

One would think these staking trips would be all a person would be required to endure, but over the intervening years, several other trips had to be made. One time, the 40 Mile Mining District decided that instead of putting the claim location notice on the NE corner post, as required by the State of Alaska Division of Mining, the notice would be posted on the upper right-hand post, which in a lot of cases is the NE corner, but not always. I thought this was a great idea because it was not always easy to determine which side of the river was the NE corner, but it was always easy to determine which was the upper right-hand corner. This was supposedly approved by the State, but after a year or so, it turned out to be false. Of course, Chris and I had changed all of his posts to the upper right-hand corners. Both changes—to the right-hand corner, then back to the NE corner—were done by boat in the summertime, a much easier time to do it.

On a few other occasions, we boated through for claim maintenance purposes, refurbishing and replacing notices and flagging, another responsibility of the claim owner. The trips down the river were always a lot of fun, with the opportunity to take other people and do some mining along the way, camping in tents, and having the usual mess ups, such as boat motor problems, tears in hovercraft skirts, and articles of clothing left behind on a rock somewhere in the middle of the river.

At some point over the years, Chris decided he was no longer interested in mining. I got the claims back. I had already started accumulating more claims and mining equipment. I was back in the mining business. This time, my involvement was on a much more casual level. I leased out my 6″ dredge, other mining equipment and claims. Then, I went to visit the lessees whenever I felt like it, hanging out for days without the hard work of mining in seasons past! The word vacation comes to mind.

Finally, I realized I was not getting any younger and began selling off claims. This involved intense activity of a different nature. It was time consuming and required traveling all over the river showing claims and advertising the claims in mining journals, as well as posting flyers here and there, and word of mouth.

An aside:

Chris and I were working to remove a deadbolt lock in the spring of 2023 when a groan escaped from Chris.

I asked, "What are you groaning about?"

He said, "We have hit the wall and can't go any further because we are lacking a tool."

I asked, knowing I had installed that deadbolt, so I must have all the tools, "What tool that would be?"

He answered, "An Allen wrench."

I said, "I have those. What size do you need?"

He looked at me as though he was seeing me for the first time, then said, "I have never met a woman who knew what an Allen wrench is."

"I not only know what it is, I own two sets, and I know where they are," I replied.

After a moment, he asked, "What would Rich have said about that?"

I hope he would have said, "This kind of knowledge is one of the many valuable things you brought to the operation."

As a general summary of all these river adventures, I have to say that some variation of these events happened all the time and to everyone dredging on the 40 Mile. We each have tales to tell! What a life!

31. END OF STORY

Kurt came and went with our team over the years. He also worked for Judd and Gail (Murphy) Edgerton for four years on bulldozers, worked with other dredgers, and ran his own dredge over a span of thirty years.

Rich and I separated. During our 15 years together, he was deeply interested in all things gold including the hard work, as was I. This distracted me from the lack of respect regarding the huge amounts of money we generated. What Sylvia Plath called the loneliness of unbelonging, as he pushed me away by trying to devalue me in an attempt to justify covering his margin debts in the stock market while using my share too, finally caused me to take myself back and leave.

Gary, Joe, and Clyde also came and went in different combinations. Some are still doing a bit of mining. It was a pleasure knowing them.

In the summer of 2004, Alaska burned. Statewide, 6,600,000 acres burned, the most in recorded history, with 1,700,000 of those acres between Tok and Eagle, in what was known as the Taylor Complex Fire, the largest fire in the United States from at least 1997 to 2019. The only cabin that burned in the Taylor fire was our cabin near Chicken.

The remains of our burned cabin. 2004.

In the summers 2012 and 2013, I moved my shop from Tok to The Goldpanner in Chicken, a fabulous establishment where a person can get a sweatshirt, food, gold, a room, gasoline, good conversation on the porch with some miner in from the river for mail, RV connections, and those flush toilets.

I was trying to sell my remaining claims due to my advancing age. Being nearer to them made the process easier. I could go to the river with the prospective buyer when I needed to.

In the middle of the second summer at the Goldpanner, the young summer hires came to me saying I am a legend of the 40 Mile! Aw shucks. Nice of you to say so. Thanks, y'all. I am thrilled at the validation.

Fifteen more years passed before the 40 Mile and I were done. And yet, in one sense, we will never be done because Kurt passed away. I spread a few of his ashes at the burned-out cabin site where he had spent so many winters, a few in a flower tub outside the bar in Chicken, as well as a few in the wood stove inside the bar. Randy Raffety and I dispersed the rest off the South Fork bridge, a central hub where much of the magic happened or at least, began.

It was a breezy day. Kurt's ashes drifted around in the air, a few floating toward Roy George and his buddies, down the gravel bar, launching to go downriver. They saluted Kurt off.

I plan to meet a similar fate, becoming part of the 40 Mile River, running through gold country, with a plaque at the Tok Cemetery joining Kurt and a few other old dredgers who hung around the area long enough to form a last hang-around group out there on the memorial wall.

Does it get any better, really?

Everything is right in my world.

6+ troy ounces of fine gold in a plastic gold pan.
Picture by James Putman

32. BIBLIOGRAPHY

A comment on a book I quote frequently entitled *Gold at Fortymile Creek: Early Days in the Yukon,* by Michael Gates, Curator Collections for Klondike National Historic Sites in Dawson, Yukon: This history is "must" reading but is not in print. Relatively easy to find on Amazon, Thriftbooks, and eBay, to name a few, it has a great bibliography, opening up a literary window into the period of time and place. Most of the early historic information in my chapter entitled *40 Mile Winter Adventure,* comes from *Gold at Fortymile Creek.* It was published in 1994 by UBC Press (University of British Columbia).

These following titles are not quoted here, but they are all about 40 Mile and are also "must" reading about this area.

They Did not Come in Four-Wheel Drive: An Introduction to Fortymile History. June 25, 1976, Reprint November 2000. BLM. Terry L. Haynes.

Chicken, Alaska: Then and Now. 1984. Self-published. Caryl Hanks.

The History of Chicken, Alaska. 2005. Goldstream Publications, Wasilla, Alaska. Ingrid Seuffert. Lots of great info in a booklet.

I Don't Do Chainsaws. Self-Published. Susan Wiren. A collection of some surprisingly gourmet takes on iconic comfort foods. All from the Chicken Cafe menu.

And of course, *Tisha,* by Anne Purdy as told to George Specht. Published by Random House. Originally released 1984.

Tisha's House and the Fortymile Country by Lisa Johnson. 2008. Xlibris. A book of photos. 38 pages.

For information about mining on State of Alaska land, contact the Department of Natural Resources, Division of Mining: https://dnr.alaska.gov/mlw/mining

For information about mining on federal BLM claims, contact the Bureau of Land Management offices: https://www.blm.gov/alaska

33. CONTINUING CAST OF CHARACTERS

LYNNE AND RICHARD BURTON: Lynne was my close friend since 1980. She was the Chicken Postmaster from 1969-1986. Her husband, Richard, foreman of the Department of Transportation Taylor Highway maintenance crew, was my friend too. Their three daughters Ronna, Randi, and Renee were raised in Chicken, all becoming solid citizens. Before working on the Taylor, Richard worked on one of the huge bucket dredges used in the area by a few mining companies back in the day.

BARBARA BORG: Chicken Postmaster 1986-1991. Barbara was raised in Eagle, AK, 100 miles from Chicken even further into the wilderness at the end of the Taylor Highway. She is a lovely soul and still an important friend from a five-year period in Chicken when our lives intersected. She ran dogs and lived in a small trailer in Chicken during her postmaster years. In the winter she got to move to an insulated, winterized home on the same land. One winter she and her dog team mushed alone from Chicken to Eagle on the frozen river. So daring.

ROBIN and DICK HAMMOND: Robin is Chicken Postmaster 1993-to date. We have spent many hours over the years talking about postal usage and life in general. Her love of travel has taken her to amazing places. She has lived in her own amazing place, Chicken, for 35 years. I don't know Dick that well, but he is from a family with bulldozer claims around Chicken. He came to the area in 1972.

MIKE DEAN, JIM WARBELOW, ROSS DAVIS, and MUD SWEETEN: Four of the original dredgers on the 40 Mile. They did their dredging in the river at the mouth of Napoleon Creek until 1981. With two 8" dredges, they had a huge camp of 14, producing legendary numbers of nuggets in one of the few nugget areas of the river. They helped Lee and me immensely during the summer of 1980. Ross remained a dear friend until his death in 1991. His post-dredging work was as engineer at PBS (Public Broadcasting System) in Fairbanks, then in Anchorage.

PAULA TALLINI: Roger's wife. In 1993 she tended dredge for Roger after his diver prematurely left because he couldn't handle dredging. The following summer she bartended for Susan at the Chicken Creek Saloon, a job she loved. She has many stories about the wild times the miners had at the bar. She stated they were always respectful to her. She has nothing but fond memories of her time in Chicken. I think her most important memory was being elected Mayor of the town of Chicken by the folks at the bar and the 3-gun salute celebrating her election! Mayor Paula!

DONNIE SNYDER, ROY GEORGE, and JOHN ROBINETTE: Dredgers whose company name was Black Velvet which was embroidered on their caps, Donnie and Roy have been around since 1980, fixtures of the 40 Mile. John was an early partner.

GLENN and EARL ELLIS "SMOKY" TAYLOR: Joe from our crew, his brother Glenn and their father Smoky dredged in 1981 at the confluence. Glenn and Joe opened Taylor's Gold-n-Stones in Fairbanks after Glenn left the 40 Mile. Joe and Glenn remained important friends of mine over all these years.

ROD and BARBARA KNIGHT: Rod was a real mountain man. His wife, Barbara, was tough too but tenderhearted. Rod toughened up his kids. They ran barefoot all summer through the tundra and over gravel bars like mountain goats. He supported his family by dredging with an 8" dredge, while sometimes having Barbara on top of the dredge. He believed in working his claims without partners, allowing him to keep all the gold from his claim, thus not needing a bunch of claims to provide for partners. The guys who worked alone also had to do the tender's job, making more work. Though a loner, he was always generous with help for miners in trouble. Barbara was an enthusiastic partner and another wonderful river woman.

MIKE MARSHALL: Chris's brother

PHIL SCHMIDT

TOM DAVIS

DAVE and SONYA HATCH

MIKE DAVIS

JOE HAJEC

DEWAYNE BOWERSON

DON and JANE HART

BILL and DONNA LANCE

JERRY ARONS and PATTI KNIGHT

TERRY HEARN

GIL SHAW

JOE SMITH

ALLEN REDMON

CARTER JAHN

MIKE WEBB

RICHARD "HYGRADE" NYGARD

BOB LEE

GORDON, DARRELL and MEL JAQUES

BUD and TROY GOODALL and CLYDE BALDWIN

JAN FLORA

DEAN "HOLLYWOOD" OLIVERA

NICKY, ARKY, CHARLES and BRENDA BASS

KELLEY BURKE

BILL RUSHING and CONNIE

PAT and EVA SCOFIELD

RANDY RAFFETY and JO ANN WEBER: Randy was Kurt's dear friend who also became my dear friend. Jo is Pat and Eva's daughter and Randy's longtime partner.

CHRIS, DAKOTA, CODY, and DEAN RACE

PAT HANNEMAN

JIM WHARY

ED HANGL

JESSE BECK SR and JR

PETE BASSETT

JIM SWEARINGIN and SYDNI SWENSON

DAWN and CHUCK REEVES

KENT EDDY

KING BROWN

MATT DANCER

MATT MEYER

JOHN and KATHERINE BURNS: Homesteaders living out there year in and year out. John worked for DOT road maintenance crew becoming foreman when Richard Burton moved to Tok.

They raised their three children 13 miles from Chicken. Brenda, Will, and Buck. The cool thing about the eight kids who grew up home schooled in Chicken in the 70s and 80s was what wonderful people they became. No one got into trouble with alcohol or the law. Brenda became a veterinarian, Will and Buck live in Fairbanks. John also mined over the years.

DAVE and SUE McCALL: Owners of the Chicken Bar and Cafe when we first went out there. During their tenure, miners could take gold into the bar, where the bartender weighed out their tab on scales. Dave and Sue's twin daughters, Michele and Melissa, grew up working in the cafe, then went to Fairbanks to high school and college, becoming MDs. Dave is Lynne Burton's brother.

BILL and MARY MORRIS: Founded The Goldpanner in Chicken in 1988, then after several years, they sold the store to the SEUFFERTS, who after some years of Cat mining in the area and running the store, sold to the JORGENSENS.

BRONK and THOR JORGENSEN: These brothers do everything and then some! They own The Goldpanner, Cat mines, a vast number of river bottom claims, all kinds of real estate, and that is just in 40 Mile country. They buy gold from the miners, and they sell gas to the miners. And they even do some mining themselves. If that was not enough, The Goldpanner has the only flush toilets for 79 miles! I just cannot emphasize enough what a luxury that is!!

MIKE, LOU, and JOSIE BUSBY: Cat/hydraulic miners who own Chicken Gold Camp, the third business in Chicken. They offer aid to miners, panning to the public, food, and more.

CY and LONNIE BRAS: Cat miners from Canyon Creek, up near Boundary. Friends for life who raised their four boys at their mine in the summers. One son, Corey, is still there, carrying on the tradition.

JEFF OWEN

LARRY and JUNE TAYLOR

JOE and MONA MITCHELL: For a long time, Joe and Mona owned 120 Mainstem claims which is 30 miles of river. They leased out to miners for a percentage of the gold dredged off the claim. They were great stewards of the claims under their care.

DAVE and TERESA LIKENS
TOM and JUDY LIKENS WESTON
MARK BREECE and CHERYL CLINE
JOHN and MARY ROOP
SCOTT REED
CECIL and JAMIE COX
MIKE PATRICK
JEFF YOUNG and ANDY STAWICKI ("The Jersey Boys")
VLADIMER, PETER, PETE, and ZEE ("The Czech Boys")
RICK and HENRY DOBELEAR
RODNEY, HALLY, KENNY, and COLTON LUNG
DUTCH EBBEN
DALE WOODS, KENNY & KARLA EBBEN and CARL EBBERS
JAMES and CHARISE PUTMAN
DYTON and SCOTT GILLILAND
MIKE FORTIER
BEN FORTIER
ALICE JUDY and VIC VINCENT
WAYNE WYCA
DON "TOAD" VANDERWAL
KEN KATAIVA
JERRY and MARBELL WALKER
GUY and MARIE FICHTELMANN
SHELDON and JENNA MAIER
BEN BANEY
RON ZIMMERMAN
BRAD BRANSON
SHARON and BRYAN YOUNG
JOANIE PFEIFFER and JOHN
BOB RILEY
MIKE O'GORMAN
BELA KALTENEKKER Jr and Sr
RON HILL, LEVI KARNS, ROD TILLETSKY, JAMES "J.D." ADAMS:
These guys bought three of my claims. Ron and Levi are still
active in the dredging world. Ron's wife, KATY, and their son,
DUSTY, were out there supporting the mining.
JIM KIMBRO
JESSE and JOELL FENCE

KEN KEENA

MIKE ADAMS

DEL SIZEMORE

MAT and GINGER FONTES

BRAD FRAMPTON

ED RAHBERGER JR

GIGI LAROUX

TOM BEMIS

BOBBY FOOTE

WAYNE and LINDA DUKE

OLE and HELEN OLSON: Ole was a Cat miner on Liberty Creek for 30 years. Helen is one of my best friends, which is why I mentioned them.

JOHN ALLEN and his family.

JOHN HOYLE and DAN GIVENS

DAVE WEGNER

ROGER LARSON

LYNNDEL MORGAN

KERRY JAMES KEENEY, ED MCKENDRIE, TONY FITZWATER, DAVID "MALLARD" ELWOOD: These are four guys who were kindred spirits from our first encounter in the summer of 2018. I helped them and they helped me.

GREG DONAGHY

WILLIAM ANGELL

EMIL GRMAN

KIM and SHERRY HENRICKSON

JERRY and KIM DAVIS

LESTER and ANITA MORLANG

MICHAEL DI CHIERA

STEVE EMERICK

BRAD MOORE

BILL and OLIVE HOBART

ORDELL and TIM CROWFOOT

DAN and NANCY GROSS

JASON KRAMER

RAY DEMERS

MIKE REED

BUG FUZZ

RANDY RENFROW
JEFF MILLER
MIKE and ASTRID BETHERS
CLIFF LEACH
RANDY DUNCAN
KEVIN DETTMERING
WILLIAM "WILL" MACHOLN and SON

This list is long. Many stories of dredging are associated with every name. I either don't know their individual stories, or they weren't part of my immediate dredge experience, or they told me after I was through writing. There may be many who belong on this list, whose names I did not know. I would say if I forgot you, I am sorry. Let me know I will correct the omission from here on out.

Dredging attracted a surprising variety of people from all education levels. One had a master's degree from Wharton Business School, and another had one in microbiology. Some had professional degrees in law and medicine. Quite a few had college educations. I got a big kick out of the majors the college people had. There was a major in textiles, a couple in the medical field, geology, business, English, aeronautical engineering, and professional flight instructor, as examples.

One miner could not read but could drive the 3,500 miles from Arkansas to the South Fork bridge on the 40 Mile River in remote Interior Alaska.

Machinists, mechanics, fabricators. So many skill sets.

Gold is a remarkable metal, the pursuit of which draws people from all walks of life.

34. ACKNOWLEDGMENTS

Thanks to Joe Taylor, Wes and Randy DeVore, and Roger Tallini for allowing me to tell a few of their adventures.

Wes and Randy were always getting into situations worthy of note. The most remarkable thing is that they lived through all of those circumstances relatively unscathed when one considers what could have happened so many times. Maybe they will write a tell-all.

While looking over many 40 Mile adventures, I noticed that many notable escapades involved fire or swamping of boats.

I made many references to the winter temperatures out in Chicken because along with the isolation, snow load and super short days, the temperatures are what sets it apart from a large percentage of the world's locations. While other more southerly places might have equivalent temperatures and snowfalls now and then, the extremes do not last as long as here.

For instance, when it snows in Chicken or even Anchorage in October or November, that snow usually does not melt until spring breakup. Part of the April or May melting pile is snow that fell seven months previously.

In Flagstaff, AZ, 30" of snow fell one day the winter of '22-'23, in what is called the snowiest city in America. Within two days, the snow had melted away. Flagstaff had 163" that winter while Anchorage had 108". Anchorage had snow covering the ground from October to April while Flagstaff's melted off several times instead of piling up for months.

Numbers such as -40°F rank in the astonishing category. I felt that the temperatures of winter 1998-1999 in the 40 Mile area played an immense role in what I just wrote about and are the reason I use the temperature readings as characters and call them by name in certain circumstances.

Several friends gave me the encouragement to keep writing when I needed it, as well as being sounding boards along the way. Thanks Dan Dooley, the Steinauer/Valesquez/Houser family, Suzanne Goodman, and John and Maria Carland for being there. Maria told me when I was halfway through writing my tale, "Having lived it and written it, you should share it, but you need to tell more of the stories." At times, not wanting to let Maria down was all that kept me writing.

And thanks to the 40 Mile and the people out there, especially our gang.

Jessie Ragasa, my niece-in-law, helped me with word processing during the months June and July of 2020. She took the various chapters I had written and put them in order, along with numbering pages, setting paragraph indentations and the like, allowing me to see where I was in the process. Over the next year, due to my lack of word processing skills, I accidentally deleted certain aspects of her hard work. This made my writing more difficult, though not insurmountable, which the work was before Jessie put it into an understandable order. I owe her a great debt because her knowledge allowed me to see the potential of this book in a way I could not when it was a jumble of papers.

Maik Schluroff helped me in 2014 by setting up the word processing program. Since I had not written much at that time, his immense skills were not fully utilized. But as with Jessie, he pointed out, by organizing the word processing, where I could go with my writing. It is easier for me to see when it is all in one place, although due to my ongoing word processing, and indeed, computer skill deficiencies, all sorts of computer complications disoriented my forward progress.

Then, in 2022, in desperation stemming from an inability to find someone in Anchorage to help with the word processing, I reached out to Maik, and *voila,* he brought the magic! Thank you, Maik, for all you did. The many ways you helped rose above and beyond the ordinary. You are the best.

Thanks to my Beta reader John Carland. Thank you, John, for your time and energy. You are also the best.

Special thanks to Roger Tallini for dredging conversations with an insider's view. I had so much fun reliving life on the 40 Mile through our conversations.

Thanks also to Chuck and Dawn Reeves, Shelly Marshall, and Edward Kuzmicz for technical input.

Made in the USA
Columbia, SC
01 August 2024

39531051R00113